Design and Deliver
Planning and Teaching Using Universal Design for Learning

by

Loui Lord Nelson, Ph.D.

·P·A·U·L·H·
BROOKES
PUBLISHING CO ®

Baltimore • London • Sydney

Paul H. Brookes Publishing Co.
Post Office Box 10624
Baltimore, Maryland 21285-0624
USA

www.brookespublishing.com

Typeset by Apex CoVantage, LLC, Herndon, Virginia.
Manufactured in the United States of America by
Sheridan Books, Inc., Chelsea, Michigan.

Illustrations by Allison Posey.

The individuals described in this book are real people whose names and identifying details are used by permission, or, in some cases, are composites based on the author's experiences.

Library of Congress Cataloging-in-Publication Data

Nelson, Loui Lord.
  Design and deliver : planning and teaching using universal design for learning / Loui Lord Nelson, Ph.D., ; foreword by David H. Rose, Ed.D.
    pages   cm
  Includes bibliographical references and index.
  ISBN 978-1-59857-350-3 (alk. paper)   ISBN 978-1-59857-382-4 (epub)
  1. Individualized instruction.   2. Cognitive styles.   3. Educational technology.   4. Children
with disabilities—Education.   5. Universal design.   I. Title.

  LB1031.N365   2013
  371.33—dc23   2013019085

British Library Cataloguing in Publication data are available from the British Library.

2022   2021   2020   2019

10   9   8   7

CONTENTS

ABOUT THE AUTHOR

Loui Lord Nelson, Ph.D., is a consultant specializing in universal design for learning (UDL). She recently completed a 1-year postdoctoral fellowship through Boston College and CAST. She has focused on K–12 professional development and systems change design and is conducting research in both areas. Prior to this experience, she was the Coordinator of UDL in Bartholomew Consolidated School Corporation in Columbus, Indiana, for four years. Loui began her career as an eighth-grade collaborative teacher in Indiana and then expanded her work to focus on the needs of individuals with intellectual and developmental disabilities in the postsecondary setting and the families of those individuals. Her work is constantly informed by the lifespan experiences of these individuals.

I can remember the beginning of my freshman year in college, sitting in a huge lecture hall with 700 other sleepy undergraduates, trying to understand why we should care about *Beowulf*. The lecturer was scholarly and impressive. *Beowulf*—an epic poem originally written in an archaic Anglo-Saxon dialect that eventually morphed into English—was by all accounts a profoundly important milestone in the development of English literature. The translation we read was undoubtedly authoritative and erudite. However, at least to me, it was also impenetrable, stiff, and boring. I finally gave up and read the CliffsNotes version. (For young readers unfamiliar with CliffsNotes and their role in college survival, ask your parents.)

Decades later (actually, in 2001), Seamus Heaney produced an equally authoritative but also vivid and startlingly captivating new translation of *Beowulf*. It was an immediate triumph. An Irish poet himself—and the winner of the Nobel Prize—Seamus Heaney was just the right person to breathe new life into the historic "chestnut." Where previous translations had gotten the words right, and even the story right, Heaney also got the poetry right. His translation succeeded because Heaney was deeply rooted in the cultural and linguistic history from which *Beowulf* had sprung, but he was also, like *Beowulf*'s author, a poet. His translation was not just a careful transcription, it was a work of art that cracked opened the meaning and emotion in an ancient poem for 21st-century audiences.

I wanted to begin with Heaney's triumph of translation because I want to emphasize the power, and the art, of good translation. This book by Loui Lord Nelson is in most senses a "translation"—a brilliant translation—of the principles and practices of universal design for learning (UDL) for the most important of modern audiences, our teachers. Like Heaney's artful translation, moreover, her book is far more than a simple translation of the language or principles of UDL. It is a wholly original work that will bring new meaning, and new audiences, to the theory and practice of UDL. Hers is a translation that, like Heaney's, is at the same time authentic and artful: It captures both the science and the art of UDL.

Three things about this book stand out for me—each echoing one of the core principles of UDL. It is no accident that these principles emerge so prominently as the underpinning of her book. She gets the most important things right.

First of all, Loui *knows* UDL. Like Seamus Heaney, who had deep knowledge of the culture and language of Anglo-Saxon England before he translated *Beowulf*,

Loui has deep knowledge about the theory and practice of UDL; she understands it thoroughly. Most important, her knowledge comes not just from books and journals but from her own experiences in real classrooms and with real teachers. She sprinkles that experience—hers and theirs—generously throughout the book. As a result, Loui's translation speaks with a clear and authentic voice; written by a teacher, with other teachers, and *for* other teachers.

Second, Loui knows how to *express* UDL. There are many who write *about* UDL, but not so many who write *with* UDL. Loui's book is not only a wonderful exposition of UDL, it is a wonderful *expression* of UDL. There are "multiple representations" everywhere that recognize and anticipate the enormous individual differences in her expected audience: she begins her book by providing (and guiding) choices in how to navigate and structure one's journey through the book; she provides multiple representations of not only the language of UDL but also its concepts in text, illustrations, charts, models; she provides not only vivid descriptions but also adroitly uses many examples (and nonexamples) as helpful alternatives to exposition; she highlights critical features in a variety of ways, she provides many different entry points for novice and expert alike, she frequently begins with a lot of scaffolding, then gradually releases the support; she prepares the reader, guides them, and provides opportunities for reflection. The book "feels" like a regular book on the surface, but the universal learning design is in its DNA.

Finally, Loui knows how to *engage* her audience. Partly it is in the voice she adopts—it is personal rather than distant, didactic, or imperious. Partly it is the gentle and gradual mentoring she provides. She greets new readers as they are, encourages taking "small steps," using what they already have and know, recognizing the ongoing demands that teaching requires. Partly it is the authenticity of her examples—they are never perfect but always approachable and encouraging. Most important, I think Loui speaks to teachers with respect, even admiration. She doesn't demean the vital role of teachers by proposing "scripts" to follow studiously or with lifeless procedures and checklists. She recognizes that teachers are best when they are thinking. Finally, she recognizes the central role of affect and emotion in any kind of teaching and learning. She writes and illustrates not just the meaning of UDL but the art and emotion of UDL. Her own writing is engaging, personal, reflective, and hopeful. There is a voice in what she writes, and it is the voice of an interested (and interesting) fellow traveler.

In short, what makes Loui's book effective is the "teacherly" way it exposes UDL—not as a lecture, a formula, or a script but as a way of thinking. Her "translation" of UDL shares much with Seamus Heaney's translation of *Beowulf*—it is authentic and knowledgeable and clear in its expression. Most important, however, it accomplishes all of that without losing the essential poetry of what teachers do.

David H. Rose, Ed.D.
Founder and Chief Education Officer
CAST

This book, like any good lesson, has a goal. That goal is to provide the reader with a solid understanding of universal design for learning (UDL) so that person can develop effective lessons. Getting to that point, though, requires the designer to consider a framework, the learning environment, and the goal of the lesson. That's quite a path to travel.

To reach the goal, this book uses quotes, illustrations, scenarios, and stories as examples. It is also written in first person. I wanted the topic to be approachable and for the book to read more like a conversation than a lecture. The structure of the book was also designed to promote choice.

This book has three sections. Section I introduces you to UDL by introducing the creators at CAST and the layout of the framework. Next, you will learn the vocabulary associated with UDL, and some common myths are dispelled.

Section II is a full breakdown of the three principles. Organized by the principles of Engagement, Representation, and Action and Expression, you can use the graphic organizer from Chapter 1 (Figure 1.2) as a reference point or simply move through each chapter.

Section III focuses on your available resources, designing a learning environment, developing goals, and designing lesson plans that align with the UDL framework. There is a description of a tool designed by CAST called UDL Exchange with which you can design, share, and store resources, lessons, and collections. The section ends with suggestions on how to investigate the design of your own lessons as you use the UDL framework.

I encourage you to move from section to section and chapter to chapter to fit your needs. If you are completely new to UDL, you might want to read the book from front to back. If, however, you are familiar with the principles, guidelines, and checkpoints, you might want to refresh your memory on the intent of UDL (Chapter 1) and then flip back to the third section to focus on putting to work your knowledge about the framework. The second section can stand alone as a reference during the development of lessons or units.

Finally, the outcome I hope you experience is a stronger understanding of UDL and a desire to begin using it as a guiding framework for your lessons and learning environment. As you will see, the teachers who have adopted UDL have watched their students blossom as individuals and learners. Remember to be patient as you begin this journey; be focused on your own learning goals. Start small, but start.

ACKNOWLEDGMENTS

I always have a wonderful time, wherever I am, whomever I'm with.

—Elwood P. Dowd, *Harvey*

This work was deeply informed by two communities and individuals within those communities. First, the experiences and opportunities I had during my four years as the Coordinator of UDL in Bartholomew Consolidated School Corporation in Columbus (BCSC), Indiana, truly shaped this book. My work with those public school teachers, building-level administrators, and district-level administrators caused me to look at UDL as an on-the-ground and theoretical framework. From developing training tools for teachers to my involvement in that district's system-level design, which used UDL as its overall framework for all instructional and curricular decisions, BCSC provided me with experiences that enriched my life.

The person who opened that door to me was George Van Horn, the Director of Special Education. A brilliant strategist, a dogged advocate for individuals with disabilities, and a visionary inclusionist, he exemplifies how the often siloed world of special education can create deep connections and establish honest collaboration with those in the other educational silos at a district level.

In addition, I thank Bill Jensen, the Director of Secondary Education at BCSC, for bringing me into discussions and establishing the Coordinator of UDL position as that of a leader within the district. It was he who put me in a coleadership role with the incomparable Mike Jamerson, the Director of Instructional Technology, to bring to life the philosophy of one device per student (also known as *one-to-one*). Bill, Mike, and I believed that all technology use must be focused on instruction, thus we grounded the initiative with the UDL framework.

Bill's passion for student involvement and expression has led BCSC's secondary schools to offer opportunities, experiences, and courses that always surprise visitors. Whenever I hear, "High school kids can't do that," or "Middle school kids are too immature for that," I always encourage that person to schedule a visit to BCSC; they will see their doubts shattered. This is because of Bill's commitment to the success of all students. He is a fearless leader who exemplifies that we cannot wait for future improvements in education, they must happen now.

This is not to say that the rest of BCSC falls short. Repeatedly recognized by journalists, legislators, business leaders, and national educational figures, BCSC has strong leaders in every corner who are focused on the academic and social-emotional needs of their students. Each of the teachers quoted and many of the scenarios provided in this book came from the classrooms of teachers in BCSC. I am deeply indebted to these wonderful educators. Each of these individuals truly exemplifies lifelong learning and a heartfelt need to reach every student. I have missed them all during my postdoctoral fellowship year here at CAST.

My journey to CAST was guided by my two advisors: Richard Jackson and Tracey Hall. It is thanks to Richard, Boston College, and their partnership with CAST that this postdoctoral opportunity was funded by the Office of Special Education Programs (to whom I also offer thanks). Richard and Tracey have been my constant supporters during my time here. Their interest in my work is appreciated, but they have demonstrated the more important trait of being interested in me as a person.

CAST's founding leadership of David Rose and Anne Meyer, with the added leadership of Ada Sullivan, laid the groundwork and continued expansion of UDL. Their diligent work, focused research, and dogged advocacy for expanded learning opportunities established a platform on which many of us now stand. I have accepted the charge to advocate for the implementation of UDL, and I thank you for creating such a solid base.

I had the tremendous good fortune to plan and present a series of eight day-long district-level professional developments with Grace Meo, Patti Ralabate, Rachel Currie-Rubin, and Allison Posey. The discussions about how to share the ins and outs of UDL and how to help educators come to use UDL as a decision-making framework provided a consistent process of reflection for this book. These women ask powerful questions that lead to outstanding products. Their friendship provided an additional joy. I look forward to continued work with them.

The illustrations throughout this book were created by the talented and intelligent Allison Posey. Also a former teacher, Allison's expertise in UDL created a connection between us that I'm not sure other authors and illustrators achieve. Her ability to take my written ideas and turn them into pictures was exhilarating and humbling to watch. The ebook version was heavily influenced by the information and support provided to me by two people. The videos would not have happened without the patient tutoring and guidance of Graham Gardner. The enhancements that allow the digital version to be as fully accessible as possible were based on conversations with Chuck Hitchcock and information on the AIM web site (www.aim.cast.org).

There were two people in particular at CAST who provided general support along the way. Peggy Coyne and Patti Ralabate became fast friends and reliable sounding boards. The best moments of creativity can happen during grocery store runs and lobster dinners.

Outside of these two communities are my partners at Brookes and Apex, and my family. Rebecca Lazo, my editor from Brookes Publishing, has become a friend during this process. Her experiences in publishing gave me the confidence to write in a voice that was comfortable, and her skills as an editor guided my decisions on the organization of the book. Most important, she let me ask question after question after question and always had a perfect answer. Erin Cahill was my Brookes ebook editor and shared my interest in making it as accessible as possible. She set no limits and, in fact, expanded those that I had. In addition, David Zielonka and his colleagues from Apex CoVantage celebrated my vision and ultimately brought this book to life. This book is evidence that the old guard of the publishing world has been replaced at Brookes and Apex with a flexible, consumer-focused mindset.

My final thanks go to my family. To my parents, Bill and Cathy Lord, who have always told your girls that we could do and become anything we wanted. Your love and support ground my soul. Thanks also to my sister Jennifer, who has always exemplified the act of doing and becoming while being centered. You have walked by my side my entire life. Namaste. And to my husband, Carl; your existence in my life brings me such peace and happiness. I love you.

To Sean. I was your teacher for a year. You continue to teach me.

I

INTRODUCING UNIVERSAL DESIGN FOR LEARNING

|| UDL isn't for me. It's for them.

—Laurie Martin, middle school teacher, social studies

It is a few days before your students come back to school. You are setting up your classroom and have some decisions to make. If you're an experienced teacher, you remember how former students moved through the classroom. You might or might not have classroom computers, listening stations, or a reading corner, but each require physical space and so you have to make decisions around their placement. You think about the chalkboard, whiteboard, or interactive whiteboard in relation to where your students will sit. Maybe you have a rug that designates an area for group instruction or a ministage on which students stand to give presentations. You probably have posters you hang on the walls. Some are inspirational with quotes and prompts whereas others are instructional with the alphabet, a number line, defined words, or other grade- or subject-appropriate information. You've had some of these resources for years whereas others are new. If you are a new teacher or teaching a new subject or grade, you are likely in a new space, which leads to even more decision making.

At first glance, much of the decision making in this scenario seems to focus on physical placement. For example, movement within a space and the arrangement of desks are typically classroom-management decisions, but these choices also affect instruction. So how do you make sure how you place or use your resources supports the learning of your students? I suggest the use of the universal design for learning (UDL) framework.

What Is Universal Design for Learning?

For some, it's easiest to approach UDL through examples of physical accessibility. When an environment is universally designed, it is designed to be accessible to as many people as possible. Do you have a pull-along suitcase? Do you push a stroller? You have likely used the curb cuts in the sidewalks or the ramps that now accompany stairs to many buildings. You have benefited from a universally designed environment. Have you ever pushed the square panel that activates the automatic door opener at many businesses? You have benefited from a universally designed environment. Have you ever steadied yourself using a wall rail? You have benefitted from a universally designed environment. In the first two cases, a barrier preventing access (e.g., a raised curb, a door you can't pull because your hands are full) has been removed through the addition of a support. In the other case, the potential support you might need for balance (e.g., the wall rails you see in hospitals, rails in stairwells) has been designed into the space. In these examples, barriers have been removed or minimized through the universal design of that space. UDL takes universal design's physical accessibility and expands it to make learning accessible. To make learning more accessible, you have to remove barriers.

UDL is a framework that guides the shift from designing learning environments and lessons with potential barriers to designing barrier-free, instructionally rich learning environments and lessons that provide access to all students. A rich learning environment (i.e., the location where learning is taking place) is designed around the needs of all students, not just those with an identified need

Table S1.1. Decisions with barriers versus removing barriers

creating possible barriers: Alphabet posters are hung on the narrowest wall because they visually look best there.

removing barriers: Alphabet posters are hung in a spot where learners can see them easily *and* they are consistently used as a teaching tool.

creating possible barriers: Student newspapers are kept next to the classroom door because it's easier for you to carry them in and out of the classroom and account for them. Students are expected to pick up a newspaper on the way in and stack them neatly on their way out.

removing barriers: Student newspapers are distributed throughout the classroom so learners have easy access to them. Student helpers are in charge of distributing them, counting them, and collecting them for recycling at the end of the week.

creating possible barriers: Student desks remain in rows and columns throughout the year. This way the students face you and you can see what they are doing at all times while you lecture, display information on the screen, or have them work at their desks.

removing barriers: Student desks are moved based on the structure of the lesson (e.g., collaborative work, individual work, partner work, presentations) and desired learning (e.g., students will combine their predictions of random issues to develop a group hypothesis).

creating possible barriers: Students know that each day they need to come having read a chapter, ready to take notes on that information, receive a new assignment, and begin work on that night's homework. This consistency minimizes classroom disruptions.

removing barriers: Students have access to the reading material in a variety of formats (e.g., audio, textual, digital) along with comprehension supports (e.g., supplemental audio, textual, digital information). They are expected to have comprehended the information before class and are prepared to debate with one another using prompts you provide.

(e.g., students with disabilities, students who are English language learners, students who are gifted). As students experience learning environments and lessons designed using the UDL framework, they become more independent, resourceful learners (Meyer, Rose, & Gordon, 2013). UDL shifts us to consider the classroom as an ecosystem where there is constant interplay between students, the resources, you, and the expectations of the environment. The framework is designed with all of those needs in mind.

When you make an instructionally focused decision, you center your attention on the students' outcomes. Stated another way, an instructional purpose underlies every decision you make when you use UDL to design your lessons and learning environments. Table S1.1 compares some decisions that might create barriers versus decisions focused on removing barriers.

The Beginning

Created more than 30 years ago, CAST was established by individuals in a clinical setting who began working directly with students with significant learning needs. Until 2002 the organization was known as the Center for Applied Special Technology (CAST). Now, they are simply known as CAST, Inc., or CAST. While the organization's neuropsychologists, university professors, former K–12 educators, and trainers saw significant gains in the students when they were in that clinical setting, they knew that these students would not have these same opportunities in traditional settings. In their minds, the challenges students were facing had little to do with the students' abilities because the students demonstrated their ability to be successful when provided with the tools, resources, and strategies that met their needs.

Up to this point, educators and researchers alike believed that the challenges of learning stemmed from the students. With issues ranging from significant cognitive disabilities to the inability to identify words on a page, the barrier to learning was seen as the learner's problem. Upon reflection, CAST asked the following:

- What if educators removed barriers at the onset when designing a learning environment, curriculum, or lesson?

- What if teachers were provided with the latest information on brain research in a way that they could apply that information within the classroom?

At that point, the founders of CAST began their work of identifying universal structures that would support the learning of all students in any learning environment.

As I stated previously, UDL is a framework. It is neither a curriculum nor a checklist. If it were either one of those things, it would oversimplify the act and professionalism of teaching. As an educator, you have taken courses in pedagogy, classroom management, and theory. You have a collection of tools, resources, and strategies you have either learned recently or over the years. The structure of UDL guides you to actively, attentively, and purposefully pull from that collection. It also asks you to possibly think differently.

The Difference

Because UDL is a framework versus a curriculum, teachers are in full control when designing the learning environment and lessons. UDL helps teachers make informed choices about everything from what posters to put on the walls to what strategies, resources, and tools they will use to teach a lesson. This is very different from structures that ask you to perform a specific list of tasks or tell you to design lessons with a narrow scope.

So, is UDL one more thing for teachers to do? In one way, it is. You will be using a framework to investigate the learning environment you're creating and the lessons you're designing. That will take time. And you might find that you need to make changes to your learning environment or the lessons you are creating. That will take time. But if you're using the framework, you will be prompted to choose tools, resources, and strategies that reach out to all of your students.

> To me, even though it was overwhelming at first and seemed like more, more, more, it's really less. The more you use it, the less challenging it is, and the more freeing it is. All of that together, I've really been excited about it.
>
> —Kathy Denniston, fifth-grade teacher

Once you become more acquainted with the framework and learn to apply the options it suggests, students will become more independent within your learning environment and your planning will become more streamlined. What you will likely notice is that you already offer a few, some, or many of the options suggested within the UDL framework. The challenge is for you to 1) ask and answer *why* you choose those options and 2) identify what other options need to be partnered with what you're already doing to ensure more students can fully participate in your learning environment.

THE SECTION

This section has two chapters. The first begins with suggestions on how to approach your own use of the framework. This is followed up with an introduction to the framework of UDL. The second chapter identifies and clarifies the terminology associated with UDL. Education is full of jargon, but the vocabulary of UDL involves mostly known terms. Though brief, this section provides the foundation to UDL. If you are familiar with this information, I encourage you to skip to Section II, where the principles, guidelines, and checkpoints are more thoroughly discussed. If the description of the learning environment at the beginning of this section introduction made you want to hear more about designing a learning environment, skip to Section III.

I know it works because my kids come in happy and ready to go. We talk about getting kids to come to school and getting them excited about learning. Teaching using UDL does just that. It would be good for teachers new to UDL to start with paper/pencil planning with the framework right there, but after a while you go away from it and it becomes natural. You see the scores going up. The kids love learning.

—Krea Hill, first-grade teacher

1

INTRODUCING UNIVERSAL DESIGN FOR LEARNING

> Why use universal design for learning? Because teaching is all about diversity and it's all about so many multiple approaches. Diversity is what every school presents. There are a variety of students and there's really no overlap between them. To be successful, there can't be any other approach but to be more diversified in whatever we're doing. I think the only hope of having everyone involved and learning is to offer those multiple choices and those multiple approaches.
>
> —Robin Whited, English literature teacher, high school

Our classrooms are nothing but diverse. Even if all of the students come from the same small community, are of the same ethnic, social, and economic backgrounds, we know that each of them has a unique, specific learning need (Rose & Meyer, 2002). So, how do we design lessons and learning environments that can support these differences? Just as Robin suggests in the opening quote in this chapter, the best way is to use the universal design for learning (UDL) framework. Once you understand how the framework is organized, become familiar with the vocabulary, and think through some processes on how to use that framework, putting UDL into action can become automatic.

> I've been using the principles for so long, it's automatic. When I'm planning, I'll go back and check, but I always include those things because it's become second nature to me.
>
> —Dana Calfee, science teacher, middle school

There is no denying that teachers are searching for ideas and strategies that will help them teach all of the students in their class while remaining in line with local, state, and federal educational guidelines. Teachers have a prescribed amount of time to deliver the content and assess whether the students are successfully meeting the specific standards, which for many are the Common Core State Standards. When students' outcomes are not aligned with the selected lesson standards, teachers have to make choices about additional supports, resources, and strategies, including how and when they will put them into action and figure out whether or not they are helping the students. To do all of this effectively, teachers must begin with the design of where they provide instruction and the design of the lesson. And whether it is the design of the location or the lesson, the design needs to be supported by an underlying strategic and evidence-based approach. This is exactly what the UDL framework supports.

This chapter introduces you to UDL. I describe the UDL framework and give you an overview of the UDL process, and although it seems it would be great to jump right in, I would like for you to consider taking on UDL slowly.

FOUR BIG THINGS

Think about what you want the end result to be. What do you really want them to learn? How are you going to represent it different ways? What choices are you going to offer? And with a teacher new to this, I would say, do not take on this whole thing. Take it in small steps. It's a matter of slowly integrating. Don't overwhelm yourself.

—Patrice Goble, fifth-grade teacher

Beginning Slowly

As teachers, we are used to taking on multiple tasks, challenges, initiatives, and programs. Sometimes it can feel as if we are stuck in a revolving door. So, considering something as big and flexible as UDL can be overwhelming. It can easily feel like "one more thing," and as you begin to learn more about the framework throughout this book, you could easily get caught up in the seemingly unending options suggested. Rather than getting overwhelmed by these suggestions, however, consider identifying which of these options you are already  touching. Get excited by the ways in which you can enhance your teaching space and lessons. Identify the parts of UDL that make sense to you. Dissect it. Pull the framework apart to find suggestions that enhance your students' learning; if that seems time consuming and overwhelming, consider other ways to approach your new relationship with UDL:

- Focus on one of the guidelines and select tools, resources, or strategies based on that guideline (see more in Chapters 3, 4, or 5).

- Focus on one of the principles to begin a general examination of your lessons and classroom/environment (see more in Chapters 3, 4, or 5).

- Begin your lesson development by asking, "How does this activity connect back to my lesson goal?" (see more in Chapter 7).

- Review yesterday's lesson using the information you learn about the principles (see more in Chapters 3, 4, or 5).

- List the different tools and resources to which you already have access. Remember to think about things and people. Now, consider how those tools and resources can help you put one or more of the principles into action (see more in Chapter 6).

- Talk with fellow teachers about the principles and guidelines and how they approach UDL.

- Do the same activities, but use that same list of tools and resources to think about one or more of the guidelines.

We vary in our learning needs just as much as our students do. In this chapter you will learn about our brain networks and how they affect our learning. Those brain networks exist in children and adults alike. I suggest that you see how you fit into the framework as a learner. Look for options that fit your learning preferences and needs. It is likely that those preferences and needs guided your initial lesson development practices. Maybe they still do.

As this book unfolds, you will have the opportunity to consider all of the different ways learners can be brought into a lesson and how you can maintain their attention and steer them toward self-guidance. You will examine the ways our brains take in information, organize it, and comprehend it. You will reflect on the ways your students take that same information and demonstrate what they know about it. More than that, though, you will think about your students as strategically minded, goal-setting individuals who can grow in their capacity to examine their own learning needs. A lot, isn't it? That is why you must choose your own entry point into UDL and start small.

A Continual Process

UDL is a process. A process is a series of actions that lead to a particular result. In the case of UDL, the series of actions include the design of the space in which you teach the lessons you lead. The particular result you are seeking is improved student outcomes. Because the particular result is student outcomes, this becomes a continual process.

Take, for example, professional musicians. These talented people participate in the process of performance. They practice a certain piece for weeks or months, knowing that they will perform that piece for a particular audience on a particular date. The result they are seeking, however, is not to play for that audience. The result they are seeking is a performance that matches their standards and desires. Critics will sit in the audience and proclaim whether or not the performance was a success, but the musicians know that the process is bigger than that single performance. The process is their continual desire to improve the outcomes of their performance.

As you learn more about UDL, you will realize that there is no defined finish line or point of completion. The arrow just keeps flying. UDL is designed to guide you and allow

for flexibility within the space you teach and within your lessons. A popular question is "When will I know I am doing UDL?" I suggest that we shift that question. UDL is not something you necessarily do; UDL is something you use to design. The question becomes "When will I know I have used UDL to its fullest?" The answer is, when you have made conscious decisions to design your teaching space and lessons using tools, resources, and strategies that align with the options suggested within the framework. When you clearly identify the goal for your lesson and connect the subsequent activities with that goal. When you realize that by using the options suggested within the UDL framework, you are opening the doors to students who are not typically included in traditional designs. Because you have opened those doors, you are truly reaching all students (CAST, 2012b).

All Students

This book does not delineate between certain student groups. UDL is based on the science of our brains and the knowledge that how we learn is as individualized as each snowflake that falls. CAST's chief education officer and cofounder, David Rose, points out that there is no such thing as an "average learner" (CAST, 2012c; Hall, Meyer, & Rose, 2012). Instead, we are not only unique in comparison to one another but we also uniquely approach learning, depending on our own response to the environment and the activity.

As a way to define additional supports and resources for some students, our educational system has grouped them. UDL is not blind to the fact that there are students who require significant support to participate, gain knowledge, and demonstrate their own knowledge. Instead, UDL suggests that you seek to design the space in which you teach and the lessons you provide using the variety of options suggested within the framework. Then, implement those options and reflect on your students' participation and outcomes. Using that information, you move forward with the same or other options suggested within the framework.

At its heart, UDL is about providing consciously selected and researched options to all students so they can ultimately learn to guide their own learning. The term *lifelong learner* describes this kind of desired outcome and is popular in education. It is up to us, though, to provide structured environments and lessons that strategically support our students in their movement toward that outcome, or many will not get there.

All Subjects

The design of UDL is such that it can be applied in any instructional setting. No matter your subject area, you make instructional decisions. The UDL framework's connection to how we learn versus a connection to a specific set of theories or types of practice allows it to be used in all settings. Throughout this book you will read about the use of UDL to design a variety of lessons and settings. The danger here is that these examples can narrow your exploration of UDL. Written with the intent to provide something concrete, the examples also require you to generalize the information to see how it fits with your current teaching assignment and experiences. I have worked with teachers across K–12 subject areas, including teachers within career preparation courses (e.g., certified nursing assistant training programs, radio and television training programs, law enforcement studies); teachers of high school science, technology, engineering, and mathematics (also known as STEM) courses; middle school media specialists; and elementary music and art teachers, all who used the UDL framework to design their space and their lessons.

INTRODUCING THE FRAMEWORK

UDL is a framework, which means it is an organized collection of big ideas that lead to providing options. While the frame is defined, and you should strive to work within it, there are a multitude of options within the frame. This is very different from structures that ask you to perform from a specific list of tasks or tell you to design lessons within a narrow scope. The ideas within the UDL framework came from educational research, educational psychology research, neuropsychological research, and brain research. By making classroom and lesson-based decisions that correspond with the organized ideas within the framework, you know you are meeting the varied needs of each learner.

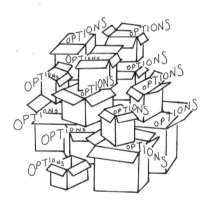

The UDL framework is organized by three areas: 1) the principles, 2) the guidelines, and 3) the checkpoints. Like an outline, the principles of Engagement, Representation, and Action and Expression name the three overarching groups and would be listed with Roman numerals I, II, and III. Under each of those three overarching groups are three guidelines, so each Roman numeral would have an A, B, and C under it. The checkpoints fill out the outline, placing anywhere from three to four points under each of the capital letters (see Figure 1.1). Another way to think about the organization of the UDL framework is the way CAST shows the information organized into three columns (see Figure 1.2). Figure 1.3 shows this same framework

I. Principle
  A. Guideline
    • Checkpoint
    • Checkpoint
    • Checkpoint
  B. Guideline
    • Checkpoint
    • Checkpoint
    • Checkpoint
    • Checkpoint
  C. Guideline
    • Checkpoint
    • Checkpoint
    • Checkpoint
II. Principle
  A. Guideline
    • Checkpoint
    • Checkpoint
    • Checkpoint
    • Checkpoint
  B. Guideline
    • Checkpoint
    • Checkpoint
    • Checkpoint
    • Checkpoint
    • Checkpoint
  C. Guideline
    • Checkpoint
    • Checkpoint
    • Checkpoint
III. Principle
  A. Guideline
    • Checkpoint
    • Checkpoint
    • Checkpoint
    • Checkpoint
  B. Guideline
    • Checkpoint
    • Checkpoint
    • Checkpoint
  C. Guideline
    • Checkpoint
    • Checkpoint

Figure 1.1. Outline example.

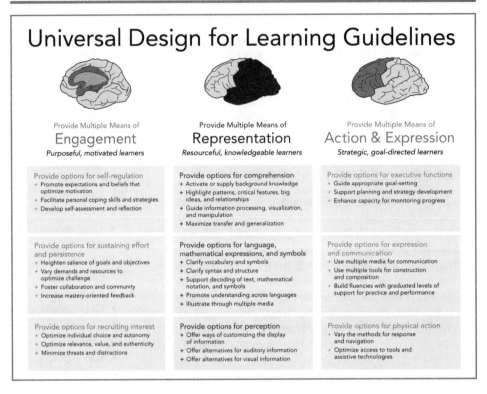

Figure 1.2. Universal design for learning guidelines.
From Meyer, A., Rose, D.H., & Gordon, D.T. [2013]. *Universal design for learning theory and practice.* Wakefield, MA: National Center on Universal Design for Learning; reprinted by permission.

with the definitions for "principle," "guideline," and "checkpoint" defined within the left column. These three examples provide you with a visual representation of the entire framework, but on what is it based?

THE PRINCIPLES AND THE BRAIN NETWORKS

As previously mentioned, the framework comes from research about our brain networks and how we respond, learn, and create. When the brain is viewed using specific technology (e.g., brain imaging), scientists know that certain connections or networks light up when stimulated. Researchers are now identifying which networks coincide with learning versus those that do not. UDL pulls together guiding ideas so teachers can create learning opportunities that activate those different learning networks. The UDL framework helps teachers determine which tools, resources, and strategies will activate their students' brain networks. Later in this chapter, I describe how the principles are framed and defined by the brain networks. Additional information about the brain networks can be found at the beginning of Chapters 3, 4, and 5.

Engagement

The principle of Engagement brings together the affective networks. These networks regulate our interactions with anyone and anything outside of ourselves. Your

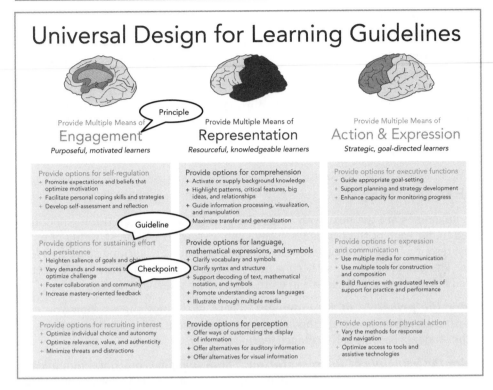

Figure 1.3.   Universal design for learning guidelines with captions.

From Meyer, A., Rose, D.H., & Gordon, D.T. [2013]. *Universal design for learning theory and practice.* Wakefield, MA: National Center on Universal Design for Learning; adapted by permission.

affective networks are active in all situations and affect how you view any situation, and since no two people are alike, how one person's affective network responds to a situation or setting will vary from how another person's affective network will respond to the same situation or setting. How we interpret any person or situation significantly affects our ability to learn, remember, and respond (Rose & Meyer, 2002). The affective networks are described more in Chapter 3.

Representation

The principle of Representation brings together the recognition networks. These networks allow us to identify and interpret what comes to us through our senses (e.g., sight, sound, touch, smell, taste). They help us find meaning in the concrete and the abstract, the simple and the complex. When we recognize an apple, interpret a painting by Picasso, smell pipe tobacco that reminds us of our grandfather, or make a single recipe 10 different times hoping to taste the same dish our mother made, we are using our recognition networks. The recognition networks are complex and are spread throughout the brain. Finally, how our brains and bodies interact with any sensory input affects how we learn (Rose & Meyer, 2002). The recognition networks are described more in Chapter 4.

Action and Expression

The principle of Action and Expression brings together the strategic networks. These networks help us strategize every physical and mental process we perform. This is where we think about what we are going to do, do what we thought about doing, and keep track of what we are doing. These are three things we do all day, ranging from brushing our teeth to planning lessons to deciding which pair of jeans to wear on the weekend. Our ability to strategize and the strategies we choose affect how we communicate to others what we know and understand (Rose & Meyer, 2002). The strategic networks are discussed more in Chapter 5.

THE GUIDELINES

The guidelines are the next level below the principles. There are three guidelines listed under each of the principles. They support teachers' understanding of what tools, resources, and strategies to choose when designing a learning space and lessons. The guidelines give further meaning to the principles and are briefly introduced below. They are discussed in more depth in Chapters 3, 4, and 5.

Under the principle of Engagement. These guidelines suggest how you can prime the students to learn, hook them into the lesson, and provide structures so the students become self-managed learners.

Under the principle of Representation. These guidelines broadly communicate what students need to learn by defining and explaining language, syntax, and numbers and by giving students opportunities to absorb knowledge in their own way.

Under the principle of Action and Expression. These guidelines suggest how students can fully communicate what they know through action, include the use of no-tech, low-tech, and high-tech materials, and allow students to practice how to plan, retain attention, problem-solve, reason, initiate and monitor their own activities.

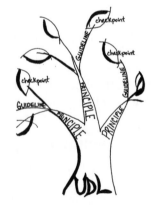

Another way to graphically demonstrate the principles, guidelines, and checkpoints is a limbed tree. The trunk represents UDL as a whole. Out of that trunk grows three limbs. These limbs represent the three principles. Out of those limbs grow branches, which are the guidelines. The leaves, fruit, and flowers supported by the branches represent the checkpoints. These support a multitude of ideas that go into the lessons you create.

A UNIVERSAL DESIGN FOR LEARNING DESIGNED ENVIRONMENT

Make sure you realize that you cannot teach one way and expect everyone to get it or assign an assignment and expect everyone to do it the same way. Just like in staff meetings. Some people take notes and others can remember the information by just listening. There are different ways that you grasp information. Kids are not that different from us; they process the information differently.

—Kandice Castillo, fifth-grade teacher

At this point, you have been introduced to the brain networks, the principles, and the guidelines. A general understanding of the UDL framework, though, can initiate even more questions. For example, "What does UDL look like in the classroom?" is a question I hear. Because no two classrooms will or should look alike, there is no single or definitive answer to this question. Instead, as you get to know the framework better and begin picking and choosing tools, resources, and strategies based on that framework to design the learning environment, you will know you are implementing UDL. Implementing UDL means you are asking and answering *why* you are choosing specific tools, resources, and strategies while designing your learning environment and lessons. Part of answering that *why* is that you are creating an environment with as few barriers as possible.

I am emphasizing the environment because the environment is where your instruction takes place. Below there is a more in-depth definition of learning environment, and Chapter 6 begins with a full discussion about the learning environment as it relates to the creation of lesson goals, but initially it is important to understand that the key to creating a UDL-designed environment is to use the framework to design your teaching space and your lessons.

Even though there is no one right way to use the UDL framework and there is no single example, teachers can look at the tools, resources, and strategies they already have in their "toolbox." When you begin to understand options suggested throughout the framework, you will see that some of the things in your toolbox are a direct match, and other things limit some of your learners. You will learn how to partner those limiting options with other tools, resources, and strategies to create a UDL-designed environment and lessons. Examples that bring to life the different guidelines and checkpoints are shown in Chapters 3, 4, and 5.

To create a UDL-designed environment you need to put into action the following three components: 1) Design the space and lesson using the framework, 2) implement that lesson, and 3) reflect and redesign the space and lesson based on the outcomes. These points are discussed in the next section of this chapter. Without these three steps, you will not have fully implemented UDL in your classroom. With these three steps, you can confidently design UDL-based lessons.

THE UNWIELDINESS OF UNIVERSAL DESIGN FOR LEARNING

So far, you have looked at the organization of the framework and learned a little about the terms of principle, guideline, and checkpoint. There are three things that have to happen before you can say you are using UDL to design your environment and lessons, and those three things are challenging to measure.

Sometimes I'll go right to an online product or approach or software or some strategy that I know is available, and then I'll work back from that. Okay, here's something that I know students have found engaging in the past, or it really demonstrated something well. How can I reuse it? Redirect it? Because I've created a menu of choices over the years, I can go back to that and make choices and selections knowing what the UDL principles ask.

—Dana Calfee, science teacher, middle school

DESIGNING

Focusing on the first component—designing the environment and lesson using the framework—you can see that you will need to become familiar with the framework, and because UDL is a framework full of choice and flexibility versus a scripted curriculum or narrowly defined teaching strategy, it can seem a bit unwieldy. There is no statement indicating how many checkpoints or guidelines should be used in the design of your learning space and the execution of the lesson. What *is* stated is that the guidelines you choose should always connect to your goal (Lapinski, Gravel, & Rose, 2012).

The concept of designing a space might be unfamiliar to some. Also called the *learning environment*, the space in which your students are learning needs to be designed so that students know they can learn there, feel welcomed while learning there, are able to learn there, and are given opportunities to express what they have learned there. The guidelines were designed to take into account the way the brain responds to the environment and information. Using these guidelines, discussed more specifically in Chapters 3, 4, and 5, will help you make these crucial design choices.

As you become more informed about and comfortable using the UDL framework, you will begin to see how the different guidelines come to life in your learning space and lessons, and the impact they have on your students. You will use informed decision making to choose the tools, resources, and strategies necessary to create a lesson designed to fire the different brain networks.

UDL is the answer to what we already know; one size does not fit all. Sometimes we think we are creating lessons that will definitely reach all of our students. We might design a lesson that might sound UDL-ish. After all, it is not straight lecture, so we must be using UDL.

Consider this scenario: Anthony's lesson was about adding integers. Because this was the first day of the topic, he found a short cartoon video in which the characters were numbers and talked about what it meant to be an integer. It showed them sitting on a number line and how they combined through addition. He gave each student a number line to use and keep in his or her folder and then followed up with a worksheet. Students worked independently, and he went to their desks if they had questions.

This sounds like a UDL lesson, doesn't it? Anthony had a cartoon video, so the students must have been engaged. Add to that the use of the number lines at their desks, and he must have been representing the information to them. Then they worked on a worksheet. That's expression, right? This must be a UDL lesson!

Let's interview Anthony about this lesson.

Loui: "Hi, Anthony. Thanks for answering some questions about your lesson."

Anthony: "Sure thing!"

Loui: "I'm curious why you chose that video."

Anthony: "We all know kids love the cartoon videos, and I thought the cartoon did a great job of introducing integers."

Loui: "It did look like they enjoyed it. Now, you followed that up with some additional instruction, and then the students worked on their worksheets. Can you tell me why you chose those activities?"

Anthony: "Well, I always follow a video with some lecture. Otherwise, I'm not teaching, right? The students have to hear and see me teach or else I'm not doing my job. Then I wanted to see if they were getting it, so I gave them the worksheets. I needed some more scores for the grade book, and those need to be individual scores. This way, I can show where they started and then how much growth they have achieved in the next two days as we work on integers. I can't get those scores from group work because that's not fair to all of the students."

Anthony's answers demonstrate traditional thinking around lesson planning. There are teachers who, like Anthony, recognize the need to hook students into a lesson. After that, the decisions are based on their own tools, resources, and strategies but not *why* they used those tools, resources, and strategies. Ultimately, Anthony did not link the design of his lesson to a goal nor did he allow that goal to guide what tools, resources, and strategies he chose.

In another interview, Anthony might point to his video as a form of engagement, and he would be correct that he touched on that principle. He did not, however, start with a goal or continue the use of Engagement. He did not seek ways to round out his lesson with additional connections to that principle or to the other two. To use the UDL framework means to use it as a planning tool. A UDL-based lesson is intentionally designed and brings to life the principles and guidelines. Anthony's story will show up in Chapters 3, 4, and 5 to help illustrate the difference between traditional lesson development and lessons designed using the UDL framework.

Maybe you have experienced the following in your teaching: A core group of students do well, but these are the students who usually do well. Another group always works ahead. When they are done they get to choose a book from the shelf, work on another project, or they bug the other students. Then there are those students who always struggle. Some of these students have individualized education programs and others struggle for other reasons. Even though you have seen outcomes like this multiple times, why do you want to change the way you design your lessons? Likely, there are a variety of reasons.

- Maybe you need to reach more of your students. The UDL framework is designed to address this wide variety of learners.

- You have plenty of tools, resources, strategies, and tips, but which ones do you choose? The UDL framework becomes a guide for decision making. It helps you choose the best tools, resources, strategies, and tips from your collection and helps identify where there are holes in your lessons.

- You are overwhelmed by varying needs and strengths of your students. The UDL framework allows you to design a classroom or learning location that fluidly meets those needs and builds on those strengths.

- You are overwhelmed with the amount of time it takes to design lessons. The UDL framework takes time to learn and adjust to. However, those teachers interviewed for this book report that they are no longer spending time choosing between tools, resources, and strategies. Instead, they make confident choices, implement with a critical eye, and reflect on the lesson.

You can read more about lesson development in Chapter 7.

If you can't shift and get to where the kids are while you're teaching, you're going to miss some kids. Because we've done our planning using UDL, we have a better idea of where to go and what to do if we need to bring kids back on track during the class.

—Libby Arthur, world history and sociology teacher, high school; social studies department chair

THE ACT OF TEACHING

The second component I mentioned was implementing the lesson. This sounds very straightforward, especially if you are an experienced teacher. You have your lesson plan, you have your tools, resources, and strategies in mind, and so you teach. UDL prompts you to do more than that. UDL asks you to be watchful of your students during the lesson and be flexible so you can meet their learning needs. In the following scenario, you will read how one teacher used the UDL framework to quickly and spontaneously check on her students' understanding of a concept.

Rhonda, a seventh-grade science teacher, was out of the classroom on Monday and had a substitute teach her lesson on diffusion. When she came back on Tuesday, she needed to quickly assess her students' understanding of the concept. She asked, "What is diffusion?" to which her students unenthusiastically responded, "When something moves from an area of higher concentration to an area of lower concentration." Although the answer was correct, she was not satisfied that they had truly taken hold of the information.

She made an instant decision to take them outside, put them into groups of six, and had them stand within the six-foot by six-foot squares created by the sidewalk seams. They then physically demonstrated for her their understanding of displacement by clumping together and pretending to be the solution added to the liquid. She then asked them to physically represent what it would look like during the process of diffusion. What she was looking for was an equal distribution of their bodies within the designated areas. Students provided each other with redirection and clarification to make sure they all understood the concept. This 10-minute attention-getting assessment introduced the lesson, reconnected the students with what they had learned about displacement, and gave Rhonda the information she needed to build on their current knowledge.

This brief activity actually gave time back to her students. She provided all of them the opportunity to

- Activate their brains, collaborate, and self-assess their knowledge (Engagement);

- Perceive displacement through physical movement, work with the language, and use what they had learned the previous day to participate in the activity (Representation); and

- Learn about displacement through physical movement, participate in an activity to build vocabulary, and use that information within scenarios (Action and Expression).

When they went back into the classroom, the students transitioned into the next activity easily. They were comfortable with what they had learned and could focus on the next task. Rhonda's students were ready to take in additional information because they had comfortably connected to the topic (Fredrickson & Branigan, 2005).

A significant piece to this scenario is the teacher. Rhonda is an experienced teacher with multiple tools, resources, and strategies in her mental and physical collection. Rhonda also knows the UDL framework so well that she can organize those tools, resources, and strategies at a moment's notice to develop an instant minilesson grounded by UDL. She knows why she needs to create that on-the-spot minilesson (i.e., hit the different brain networks) and has a mental checklist of what she needs to do to make sure all of the students gain from the experience. The students respond well because they are used to an interactive, collaborative environment in which everyone's participation is important and necessary to everyone else's learning. Most importantly, Rhonda understands and demonstrates that every student needs to feel that they are a valuable and integral part of the learning process. She sees an undeniable link between emotion and cognitive processing during learning (Storbeck & Clore, 2012).

REFLECTING

> I really like UDL because when you're trying to troubleshoot what the problem is or to just reflect daily, you might say, "That went well," or "This was not so great." In that case, 9 times out of 10 I can pull out the framework and say, "That was what I was trying to get to but it didn't play out right."
>
> —Dana Calfee, science teacher, middle school

The third component I mentioned is reflecting and redesigning the space and lesson based on the outcomes. Teaching should be a reflective practice. Reflection can be an independent activity, such as Dana mentions. She is a teacher who not only uses the UDL framework to plan all of her lessons but also uses it for her reflections at the end of the day. I'm sure you are like me and have always known in your gut when a lesson has gone well or when it has not, but have you been able to figure out why? Have you had any kind of guide or framework you can use to help you answer that question? Dana turns back to the UDL framework and asks, "What was the goal of my lesson," and "What did I use to get that across to my students?" She then reviews what tools, resources, and strategies she made available to the students and identifies where the holes were that she can fill next time.

Another reflective strategy I find to be valuable is the collaborative method. As an individual, you can think through why you made certain decisions while planning and teaching, but the subsequent answers and ideas come from your knowledge and experiences. When you add even one more person, you can exponentially add to your knowledge and experience base. The discussions, questions, and even disagreements with colleagues create many more opportunities for growth, change, and success in your classroom (Schmoker, 2004). One collaborative structure is professional learning communities (PLCs).

It's really important to plan together, but it's just as important to go back and talk about what worked and what didn't work.

—Tracy Wise, learning resource teacher, middle school

PLCs have become a popular collaborative structure within schools. These are groups of educators who come together to enrich their own practice through discussion and action and can be created formally or casually. Sometimes there is an administrator involved and other times there is not. A PLC is an organized group of professionals who come together for professional learning and to participate in data-driven inquiry. The intent behind PLCs is organizational learning; the danger of PLCs is that they become too focused on accountability (Hargreaves, 2007). To help keep educators focused on the original intent of PLCs, Richard and Rebecca DuFour and Robert Eaker (n.d.) have established what they call The 3 Big Ideas of a PLC, or what PLCs should do:

1. Focus on learning

2. Build a collaborative culture

3. Focus on results

Their six essential characteristics for a PLC include the following:

1. Shared mission, vision, values, goals

2. Collaborative teams focused on learning

3. Collective inquiry

4. Action, orientation, and experimentation

5. Commitment to continuous improvement

6. Results orientation

Because PLCs are a combination of individuals, there are recognized complexities. Where some teachers stand in their use of data, what those data demonstrate, and how to effectively use those data can vary from the other individuals in the PLC. In addition, the PLC sits within the larger context of a school and community (Nelson, Slavit, & Deuel, 2012). Although these dynamics cannot be ignored, a PLC can become a strong unit of discussion and decision making that can improve student learning and outcomes.

Nelson et al. (2012) discovered that linking the data-discussion process to 1) the content and learning goals, 2) instructional practices, and 3) student understanding provided PLCs with a framework within which to gird their discussions. Furthermore, when PLCs experienced conversations grounded in inquiry, they continuously sought to find a common meaning and were explicit when expressing their statements of wonder or uncertainty. The entire group used methods to probe, clarify, and question professional assumptions and their own beliefs and practices. A trust developed within the group that allowed them to analyze deeply and come to that common meaning.

Why are PLCs helpful when putting UDL into action? It is because we all have questions and concerns about our teaching. UDL requires us to broaden our knowledge and our use of tools, resources, and strategies we may have never heard of before. If we are really going to design lessons to support the brain networks, we need to be able to reflect on our own understanding of those brain networks, how our own brain networks respond, and how we see our students reacting to our teaching.

CONCLUSION

The intent of this chapter was to ease you into UDL. As I stated at the beginning, there are a multitude of ways to enter the world of UDL; this chapter provided one of those pathways. The concept of UDL as a framework is important to understand because it helps shove other interpretations out of your mind. Like professional musicians, when you use UDL to plan your environment and lessons you are never done. There is no final pinnacle within the framework. Instead, your indicator becomes the outcomes of your students. The second chapter of this section provides definition to language already common within education but that might need clarification in concert with UDL. It ends with a discussion of six common UDL myths.

2

THE VOCABULARY AND MYTHS OF UNIVERSAL DESIGN FOR LEARNING

> Using the UDL framework made it possible for me to do a better job at what I was doing, but to make it so that students could find a way to connect differently than they had before with their learning experience.
>
> —Rhonda Laswell, former science teacher, middle school; Coordinator of UDL

Sometimes we need language to define what we already know. Sometimes we need language to consider new things. Universal design for learning (UDL) does both. You have already been introduced to some of UDL's vocabulary, such as *principle, guideline,* and *checkpoint.* You have been introduced to the brain networks, and that those networks are called the affective networks, the recognition networks, and the strategic networks. I've referred to UDL as a framework, and there are additional terms that are often used with UDL that are worth defining. These terms bring together large concepts, so they can be challenging to understand if you don't have some basic knowledge. When UDL is talked about, teachers will hear terms such as *framework, learning environment, flexible resources, the lesson goal, access, barriers,* and *learner variability.* In the next section of this chapter I list the terms, give descriptions, and provide some examples.

FRAMEWORK

UDL was not designed to be complex, but because it is a framework and not a checklist, some might find it overwhelming. In Chapter 1 I described the concept of a framework. You can also think about a framework as a three-dimensional box. Within that box are the results of the research CAST has discovered and performed, all of which uphold the principles, guidelines, and checkpoints within the framework.

Another example is a building. When a building is going up, the building is framed by steel girders. It is on that frame that the roof will sit and the materials for the walls will hang. If the framework is not solid and shifts, then the roof could fall in or the wall materials could crack. That building's framework is tested over and over by gravity and the use of the building.

The framework of UDL, designed by researchers at CAST, was conceived using brain research (Rose & Meyer, 2002). That research was grouped into the three broad principles and then into nine guidelines. Further review brought the checkpoints to life (see http://www.udlcenter.org/research/researchevidence/). Just as a structural framework is tested by gravity, the UDL framework is tested by CAST's continuous review of the research and teachers' daily use and investigation.

LEARNING ENVIRONMENT

As mentioned previously, teachers use the UDL framework to design both lessons and the learning environment. In Chapter 1 I introduced the concept of the *learning environment* as your teaching space or location. When most of us think of teaching, we think of being in a classroom. We think of a specific location. UDL asks us to expand our concept of both where learning can take place and what needs to be available for learning to take place. A learning environment includes the physical location where learning is taking place, the resources available to the students, and the design of the lesson. To implement UDL, a teacher must go beyond the basic decision making of "what topic will be my focus for today." Instead, the teacher considers the environment in which the students will learn and uses the UDL framework to design that environment so students have access to the tools, resources, and strategies they need and so that they can achieve to their greatest potential.

The Physical Location

Think about a classroom as an example of a physical location. There might be desks and chairs, tables and chairs, or desk units. In most cases, these are mobile. Depending on the physical structure of the room, these can be grouped, placed in rows, or a larger shape such as a square or circle can be created. If there are students who use mobility devices (a wheelchair, a walker, or other assistive devices), a teacher wants to be sure these students have physical access to the seating and they are physically included within the larger chair and desk groupings.

Another piece underlying several of the guidelines and spanning all three of the principles is collaborative work. Students need opportunities to debate, discuss, negotiate, and challenge one another. Without these opportunities, they do not build important positive social and higher order thinking skills (Cohen, 1994; Schwartz, 1999). This is another way the organization of the classroom can affect your implementation of UDL. Students are more likely to collaborate if you create a physical environment that supports it.

A physical location can also be somewhere outside of the classroom. Maybe you've taken the students to a museum, the zoo, or your statehouse for a field trip. Maybe, perhaps like the example with Rhonda in Chapter 1, you've taken your students outside and into the school yard. Either way, these locations have become your new learning environment. To implement UDL, you need to consider why you chose that learning environment and how you will use that physical space in concert with the UDL framework.

Flexible Resources

The term *flexible resource* is a combination of two terms and can have multiple meanings. First, there is the overall term of *resources*, which is anything teachers or students use to learn about a topic. Resources can include printed materials (e.g., books, magazines), digital materials (e.g., online information, a DVD, devices that speak, print, or otherwise work as a reader), or representative objects (e.g., a baseball, a diorama, a stuffed animal). That last category is the largest because it includes anything teachers might use to represent an object or a topic.

When a single resource is flexible it can be used in several different ways to demonstrate the same information. Using a hypothetical computer-based program as an example, let's say a student needs to read a story, but that student does not decode words well. The goal of the lesson is for the student to identify a story's characters, setting, and plot, and then predict the end of the story. Knowing that this student will spend time and effort decoding, and it is likely that this student will not meet the goal due to frustration and lack of time, the teacher sets up the computer-based program to read the story aloud. This allows the student to look up words that are unclear and gives the student the ability to use an on-screen highlighter to highlight the characters and words that identify the setting and plot, and then export that information into another document where the student can type up his or her thoughts on the plot and story predictions. Not only does this resource allow the student to hear the information, it provides writing and organizational supports. That is an example of a flexible resource because it allows the student to meet the lesson's goal while using that tool. This type of example would support the needs of English language learners, reluctant learners, and students who are not identified as having a disability but who struggle with reading. It's not as important to know why the student needs to experience this kind of flexibility; it's more important to offer the flexibility to all of your students so they all have access to learning.

Another way to interpret the term *flexible resource* is to consider how the resource itself can be repurposed or reformatted to meet the needs of the student using it. The National Center on Accessible Instructional Materials (http://aim.cast.org/) developed standards for publishers who create content files (CAST, 2012a). They are to use specific code that can be presented in different ways and styles. This means the file can be easily converted to Braille, large print, HTML, DAISY talking books, or talking books using a human voice to text to speech (CAST, 2012b). This policy applies to instructional materials published after July 19, 2006. These converted materials are available to students with print disabilities and students with low vision or blindness, but how these students qualify for these supports depends on their disability. That information can be found under Question A-3 at http://aim.cast.org/learn/policy/federal/nimas_q_and_a#students_eligible.

If you are a general education teacher, why is it important for you to know about National Instructional Materials Accessibility Standard (CAST, 2012a) and accessible instructional materials (AIM)? Isn't that the responsibility of the special education teacher? As a general education teacher, you will likely have students in your classroom that could benefit from access to these materials. And if you are implementing UDL during your lesson design and lesson implementation, then you understand how important it is for all of your students to have access to the learning materials they need. You also understand that you are part of a team of teachers who influence your students' learning. As a team member, you recognize that by working together, student learning and access to materials can improve. In addition, if you are part of a team choosing textbooks and other curricular materials then you can use this information to ensure that your students with print or vision disabilities can fully benefit from the materials. There are many strategies that have grown from AIM that every student can use. To see how AIM and these strategies have affected the lives of students, go to http://aim.cast.org/collaborate/knowledge/story and listen to students' stories.

The term *flexible resource* can mean something else. When the teacher allows the student to use a resource in a way that is meaningful to the student rather than requiring the resource to be used in a specific way, then the resource becomes flexible. Take, for example, base-10 blocks. These are three-dimensional plastic squares and rectangles that can represent mathematical concepts. Small, 1-centimeter by 1-centimeter squares can represent 1s. Put 10 of those together in a row, and you have a block of 10. There are also 10 blocks, which are sometimes different-colored rectangles that are the same height as the 1 block but look like 10 of the 1 blocks glued together. The 100 blocks are similar to the 10 blocks except they look like 100 of the 1 blocks glued together. These blocks can help students grasp the concept of decimals (e.g., the ones place, the tens place, the hundreds place), reducing fractions (e.g., a physical representation of the numerator and denominator to show how both can be reduced), and many other math concepts.

By definition, base-10 blocks can be a flexible resource. However, if the teacher always defines how the students must lay out the tiles, the resource loses some of its flexibility. The resource becomes so structured and rigid that some students cannot connect with them. For example, students are asked to demonstrate the number 123. If the teacher leaves open how the students represent the number, then the resource is being used flexibly. Students might stack their blocks, line them up like a train, group them according to 100s, 10s and 1s, or create a shape. How they lay them out does not necessarily determine their understanding. Instead, being able to tell the teacher or their student partner how they've represented the number catapults the students into a higher level of comprehension. We assume that because the student does not put a 100 block to the left, two 10 blocks in the center and three 1 blocks on the right that they do not understand the number 123. However, a brief conversation could show that the student organizes the answer differently but understands the concept. Underlying this example of flexible resources is the goal of the lesson. In this case, the students were asked to express 123 and base-10 blocks were one of the ways they could demonstrate that knowledge. The goal should always drive the lesson.

Obviously, the term *flexible resource* has several interpretations. The first example showed how a digital resource could become flexible if it supported the learning needs of a student who needed certain supports but not others. The second example discussed the ability for a print-based resource to be translated into whatever format makes it accessible to a student with a print or visual disability. The third example demonstrated how the teacher's interpretation of the resource's use made it flexible. All three of these examples depend on specific decision making by the instructional leader. Regardless of the interpretation you are using, how you design your learning environment determines whether available resources are flexible in your classroom.

THE LESSON GOAL

The goal is the heart of any lesson. All activities, resources used, and products produced should be grounded in that goal. A UDL goal has one quality: The "how" tends to be left out (Coyne et al., 2009). The goal should state what the students will learn, but when a teacher leaves out the "how," it leaves open the possibility of how the students will learn that topic. The same is true for lessons that include assessment. The goal might state that the students will be assessed, but it does not specify how the students will be assessed. To describe how the students will learn the topic or how the students will be assessed paints the teacher into a corner by limiting what resources will be used and how they will be used. By leaving out the how, teachers have more flexibility during the lesson to meet spontaneous needs or needs that weren't previously known.

What if you teach in a school, district, or state that requires you to include a "how" within your goal? You can still provide that flexibility in your goal if you use the right verbs—verbs that are broad enough to allow for multiple tasks or assessment formats. For example, your initial goal might read, "The students will write three predictions about the character Wilbur in *Charlotte's Web.*" By using the word *write,* this limits the instructional tools to paper and pen or pencil. If the teacher is focused more on the students' ability to create predictions, then the teacher could use the word *establish* instead of *write.* Thus, the ways in which the students will show their predictions is left open.

If the teacher's lesson is designed to focus on the students' ability to write using paper and a pen or pencil (with the appropriate accommodations for students with disabilities), the character of Wilbur in *Charlotte's Web* is the secondary component of the goal. Wilbur is the topic about which students will write. Patti Ralabate (2010), from CAST, created a list of these suggested verbs (see Table 2.1).

Table 2.1. One hundred active verbs you can use to write observable and measurable goals

add	demonstrate	express	propose
analyze	demonstrate use of	follow directions	question
apply	describe	formulate	read
appraise	design	identify	recall
arrange	detect	illustrate	recognize
assemble	determine	imitate	reconstruct
calculate	develop	infer	record
categorize	devise	initiate	relate
choose	diagnose	inspect	repeat
cite examples of	diagram	interact	report
collect	differentiate	interpret	respond
communicate	differentiate between	list	restate
compare	discriminate	locate	review
complete	discuss	manage	select
compose	distinguish	modify	sequence
conclude	divide	multiply	solve
construct	dramatize	name	spell
contrast	draw conclusions	operate	state
copy	employ	organize	subtract
correlate	engage in	pick	tell
create	estimate	plan	translate
criticize	evaluate	predict	underline
debate	examine	prepare	use
deduce	experiment	present	utilize
define	explain	produce	write

From Ralabate, P. (2010). *Meeting the challenge: Special education tools that work for all kids.* Washington, DC: National Education Association; reprinted by permission.

The lesson goal is also driven by the standard. Discussed more in Chapter 6, with 45 states adopting the Common Core State Standards (CCSS) at the publication date of this book, teachers will have the latitude to use their professional judgment in how to design lessons to meet the standards. The National Governors Association Center for Best Practices and Council of Chief State School Officers (2010, p. 6) state, "The Standards define what all students are expected to know and be able to do, not how teachers should teach." The new CCSS will allow for multiple pathways to the learning as determined by the lesson goal.

ACCESS

Discussed earlier, access can refer to AIM and flexible resources. But access can also refer to a student simply being able to connect to the information being taught, and keeping the "how" out of the lesson goal or broadly defining the goal makes choosing flexible resources even more important. Underlying the selection of flexible resources are the broader concepts of access and barriers. Access considers how the students connect to the lesson, how the topic is taught, and how the students express themselves. Based on UDL, access means that

- students are given a reason to emotionally attach to the lesson;

- students know they will be given a variety of opportunities to use, watch, touch, smell, maybe even taste something that will help them understand the topic better; and,

- students will have multiple opportunities to meaningfully and successfully demonstrate that they understand that topic.

When students have access to the learning environment, the teacher has considered the physical location and the resources that are used to teach the lesson while designing the lesson.

A popular cartoon demonstrates physical accessibility and how it benefits everyone (see Figure 2.1).

By shoveling the snow from the ramp first, the building is instantly made accessible to everyone standing there. The cartoon suggests that the adult needs to change his mind set to view the ramp as a way for all students to access the building rather than as a specialized support specifically for students using wheelchairs. This same analogy can be used to describe accessibility during the lesson. Going back to the example with Anthony in Chapter 1, he offered his students a cartoon video about integers and a number line. For those students who needed to process that information aloud to fully comprehend it, that lesson was inaccessible. A quick "turn to your neighbor and together list two things you know about integers" would allow these students to begin talking through the concepts. Adding the opportunity for each group to share their two items and then writing those items on the board would allow students to continue processing what they spoke with what they hear. Anthony could correct students' inaccuracies before they began their practice. Suddenly, the lesson is accessible to more learners.

CLEARING A PATH
FOR PEOPLE WITH SPECIAL NEEDS
CLEARS THE PATH FOR EVERYONE!

Figure 2.1. "Clearing the Path."

From Giangreco. M.F. [2007]. *Absurdities and realities of special education: The complete digital set [CD].* Thousand Oaks, CA: Corwin Press. Reprinted by permission of the copyright holder, Michael F. Giangreco.

BARRIERS

Barriers are those situations and structures that prohibit involvement, learning, and expression. At its most basic, a barrier is a physical separation from the classroom or lesson. The cartoon shown in Figure 2.1 also gave a great example of a physical barrier. Not shoveling the snow off the ramp is a barrier for the student using the wheelchair. The lack of a ramp, doorways that are too narrow, the lack of appropriate seating, or excessive distance from other students are other examples of barriers.

A barrier also includes when a student is removed or denied access to a learning environment. Remembering to design around the learning environment (i.e., the physical location, the resources used, and the design of the lesson) can help teachers discover barriers that could be present throughout the environment. As an example, consider a lesson in U.S. history on Harriet Tubman and other individuals involved with the Underground Railroad. The teacher assumes that all of the students learned about the Underground Railroad in eighth grade, but there are students who aren't native to the United States, were absent from school due to illness during that portion of the year, or didn't grasp the concept of the Underground

Railroad. For a variety of reasons, these students have always envisioned the Underground Railroad as a system of railroad tracks that go from somewhere in the southern part of our county to somewhere in the northern part of our country. This misunderstanding is a barrier to that student's participation in discussions, debates, and an understanding of what Harriet Tubman and others actually did.

To lessen the barrier, the teacher anticipates this confusion and introduces the lesson by talking about the "stations" or homes with cellars, closets, and false rooms, where escaped slaves hid as they traveled north. Although these are wonderful examples, some students might not have seen or heard of a cellar before. Maybe the closets in some students' homes are very small, adding to the confusion of how a person could hide in a closet; others may never have heard of a false room. Even with verbal descriptions, the lack of photos or video clips could also be a barrier to their understanding of the Underground Railroad. By referring to the UDL framework during the development of the learning environment and lessons, the teacher can consider these barriers and decide what examples and resources should be offered as background knowledge.

Barriers can also appear when the instructional leader does not acknowledge and act on the fact that cognition and emotion are interrelated (Immordino-Yang & Damasio, 2007). In fact, emotion not only modulates cognition and perception, it is also associated with a wide variety of thought processes (Stornbeck & Clore, 2012). As the instructional leader within the environment, you take the lead in setting the emotional temperature of that space. By creating an emotionally welcoming space, you have lessened barriers.

> Background knowledge is information the student currently knows and understands and can be directly linked to the information being introduced or taught.

INFORMED DECISION MAKING

When you participate in informed decision making, you are using information you know, information that is provided to you, or information you have gathered from another source. You then apply that information to your decision making. In the case of UDL, informed decision making means you are using the UDL framework to plan and implement your lessons. You are informed about the framework's principles, guidelines, and checkpoints and make your curricular decisions based on those areas. As you are learning about the framework and you are taking your first steps in implementing them, you should scaffold your own learning. See Chapters 3 through 5 to begin your understanding of the framework.

To get started with informed decision making, consider focusing on one principle or even one guideline at a time. Investigate it; discuss it with your colleagues; discover tools, resources, and strategies that support that principle or guideline; and weave them into your lesson. Be watchful. Observe whether your new focus or additional supports you've added into your lesson lead to student engagement, a stronger representation of the topic, or more breadth in how students can demonstrate their lesson.

For example, while reading through the guidelines you might be particularly drawn to Guideline 6, "Provide options for executive functions" (Meyer et al., 2013).

You like for your students to take responsibility for their work, the use of their time, and keeping themselves on track, and you have learned that executive functions are the processes that underlie planning, problem solving, and goal-driven behavior (Miyake, Friedman, Emerson, Witzki, & Howerter, 2000). This guideline resonates with you.

You begin thinking through the different ways you already support your students' executive functions. They have class calendars to help them see when assignments are coming up, projects are due, and tests will be given. While considering the calendar, though, you realize that your students don't plan out how they are going to use each day and on what goal they are focused. You decide that your students need to practice setting appropriate goals for themselves and how to determine steps and strategies to help them accomplish that goal. By consciously applying this support within your learning environment, you are moving toward the implementation of the guideline you've chosen.

While goal setting and strategizing how to meet that goal are parts of Guideline 6, you realize that you can do more to support the development of your students' executive functions. Instead of becoming overwhelmed, you turn to your colleagues and ask them for suggestions on the strategies they use. You are familiarizing yourself and your students with Guideline 6 through informed decision making. You are choosing specific strategies based on the UDL framework.

LEARNER VARIABILITY

Students learn differently. We know this. What we don't tend to realize, however, is that students learn differently not only within one environment but also across environments (Hall et al., 2012). Student learning is three dimensional.

When a learner is considered to be one dimensional, that learner is seen as a student who has a single learning preference. For example, he likes to learn on his own, preferably through reading. If we allow that same learner to be two dimensional, he now learns on his own and within structured groups, but he still prefers to read to gain knowledge. We know, however, that students move from location to location, from context to context. This makes the learner three dimensional.

How a student learns within a context depends on his or her relationship with both the environment and the instructor. As I discussed previously, the environment encompasses both the physical location and flexible resources. Learners are affected by their own preferences; they also interact with the environment around them (CAST, 2012b; Rappolt-Schlichtmann, Daley, & Rose, 2012; Storbeck & Clore, 2012).

To create a learning environment where the variable needs of all students are considered, teachers use the principles of Engagement, Representation, and Action and Expression while planning. They understand how the design of the UDL framework helps ensure experiences that embrace all learners. Although each learner is variable, teachers using the UDL framework design the learning environment so that it embraces and enriches all learners instead of designing an environment that has to be changed to meet the needs of single learners or a small group of learners. They see that a learning environment can affect learning through the design and choice of flexible resources and the creation of the lesson goal, providing access, limiting barriers, and taking into account how learners are variable not only within a single environment but also across environments.

Most teachers are familiar with and depend on the model of consistency. A learning environment that plans for variable learners might have you questioning how that design partners with consistency. Dana Hagmann, a first-grade teacher, talks about how she intertwines consistency with variability:

> We really focus on daily routines. The students strive with structure, and they are really successful with structure because they need to know what is going to go on next. And so establishing those procedures and routines at certain times of the day is something that they can count on being stable. Regardless of what is going on around them, their environment, at home, or with their peers, they can always count on the structure of the lessons I teach or the structure of the classroom to be the same. You want to meet each kid where they are within that structure and give them ways to come at the lesson, understand the lesson, and express what they know.

MYTHS

> Sure, UDL takes time because you're planning differently, but I think people make it too hard, too. Usually it's because they haven't used UDL before.
> —Kelly Stilson, learning resource teacher, high school

Because UDL is a framework, it allows for freedom and creativity in both lesson and environment design. With that freedom, though, comes confusion for some. There are myths I have heard from teachers, conference presenters, and administrators. I will dispel some of those myths here; others will be addressed more thoroughly in future chapters.

MYTH: UDL has no research behind it.

FALSE: The establishment of UDL is grounded in brain research and other empirical data (CAST, 2011). If you go to http://www.udlcenter.org/research/research evidence/, you can begin your journey through each UDL principle, guideline, and checkpoint and see the research behind them. CAST reviewed over 1,000 articles to establish the basis for their theory. The research articles make clear why each component of the framework is so broadly defined and why there are so many ways teachers can put them into action. They also clarify why each of the principles and guidelines should be considered during the design of every lesson.

Behind this same myth, there is another question. Is there research behind the use, or implementation, of UDL? No and yes. Beginning with no, the framework of UDL will be used differently in every situation. Inherent to the framework is choice. It is designed to meet the challenges presented by every different kind of learning environment. Although the definition of the principles, guidelines, and checkpoints stay the same, how they are implemented will look very different based on available tools, resources, and the teacher's knowledge of strategies. Studies that validate effectiveness vary in design, and all have limitations. I'm not going to outline the different types of design possible; rather, I'm going to first answer *no* to this question by pointing to a popular design for large-scale clinical studies. One type of educational effectiveness study design establishes specific, precisely definable, and identical activities and actions that can be identically measured. That design relies on two concepts foreign to UDL: a strictly defined version of UDL in action (e.g., a lesson designed using the framework but applied identically across different environments) and students demonstrating their knowledge using identical methods (e.g., writing by hand) while taking the exact same assessment (e.g., multiple choice). While this single example demonstrates how the implementation of UDL across an entire lesson or environment might be quantifiably measured, it exemplifies the point that the breadth, depth, and flexible nature of UDL make it a challenging framework to measure. Through the process of investigation, researchers risk weakening the application of the UDL framework and, subsequently, the learning experiences of students. It is true, however, that researchers continue to look for ways outside of this example to empirically show that UDL positively affects the learning of all students. This is where I answer *yes* to the question.

Two such studies investigated the use of digitally based resources coupled with instruction and support designed using UDL. In both studies, there was an experimental environment where digitally based resources were designed using the UDL framework and a control environment where other traditional methods were used. The teachers in the experimental and control environments were provided instruction on UDL and both studies emphasized the same core learning in experimental and control environments.

Both studies showed that the students who used the digital resources designed using the UDL framework and within environments where the teachers supported the use of those resources through lessons designed using UDL performed better on standardized measures than those students who used resources that were not developed in reference to the UDL framework (Coyne, Pisha, Dalton, Zeph, & Smith, 2012; Rappolt-Schlichtmann et al., 2007). One of these studies also explored the perceptions and experiences of both students and teachers in relation to the UDL-designed resources and found that both groups reported high levels of excitement and interest in the digital resource and students showed a higher level of ownership in their work and felt more competent in their knowledge (Rappolt-Schlichtmann et al., 2007). As these studies demonstrate, it is equally as important to choose flexible resources (in these cases, resources designed through the use of the UDL framework) *and* to design an environment and lessons that are accessible to all students.

Another way to face this myth head on is to look for ways to address your own design process. Because the framework was built based on evidence, it can lead you to best practices. Once you become familiar with the framework, I suggest these steps:

1. Identify the practice you are currently using or would like to use in your classroom.

2. Identify whether that practice connects directly to one or more of the UDL guidelines or checkpoints.

3. Identify how that practice supports your goal.

4. Identify how you can measure the success of that practice in relation to your goal.

5. Implement the practice and look at those data produced in relation to your goal.

6. Examine those data to find evidence that your students are moving toward becoming resourceful, knowledgeable, strategic, goal-directed, purposeful, and/or motivated learners.

MYTH: UDL is just differentiation.

FALSE: Differentiation is a component of UDL. Differentiation helps teachers focus on the unique levels of readiness, interest, and the learning profiles of each student. Teachers also individualize the teaching methods used, determine a criterion for student success, and define how students will express themselves (Santangelo & Tomlinson, 2009). UDL addresses the environment first. As discussed previously, the environment includes the physical location and the lesson, unit, and/or curriculum. By proactively addressing the environment, the teacher establishes accessibility regardless of strengths, needs, abilities, or disabilities. All students have full access to what is available within the environment.

MYTH: UDL is only good to use when you have students who have individualized education programs (IEPs).

FALSE: Although UDL grew out of accommodating the needs of students with disabilities, the continued review of neuroscience and classroom application has clearly identified UDL as a viable and helpful framework to use in any classroom, especially an inclusive general education classroom where students of all ability levels are present.

It is true that a teacher can make modifications and accommodations for students with IEPs or for students who demonstrate noticeably strong skills (these students might be identified as gifted). There is an inherent and common assumption, though, that the rest of the students are "general education students" and learn like each other. This is an inaccurate assumption based on the definition of variable learners. UDL has taught us that it is the environment not the students that needs to change and that every student is a variable learner. By designing a lesson that takes into account the three principles and brings to life the guidelines, the teacher has created a learning environment where most students will perform well. Additional ideas are shared in Chapter 6.

MYTH: If you purchase a UDL product, then you're doing UDL.

FALSE: UDL implementation begins with the creation of the learning environment and lesson development, not product usage. If a teacher chooses to implement a product or strategy but does not make that choice based on the principles and guidelines of UDL, then that person is not implementing UDL. As discussed previously, each of the principles and guidelines has evidence behind it. Using the guidelines to design the lesson means that the teacher is choosing tools, resources, and strategies that he or she believes will be beneficial. This also shifts the thinking from *doing* UDL to *using* UDL as a decision-making framework.

Although the product or strategy might link nicely to one or more of the guidelines, it must be partnered with other tools, resources, and strategies to fully implement UDL. If the teacher uses the framework of UDL to choose lesson strategies and activities, then the teacher can be sure accessibility is part of the design. Lesson design is discussed more in Chapter 7.

MYTH: UDL is just good teaching.

FALSE: While a person implementing UDL might be described as a good teacher, a person who is recognized as a good teacher is not necessarily implementing UDL.

I have noticed that people use the phrase *good teaching* when answering, "What is UDL?" Good teaching isn't defined, whereas UDL is a defined framework with principles, guidelines, and checkpoints. The term *good teaching* has no agreed upon definition.

The danger of simplifying UDL as good teaching lies in two points: individual experiences and individual values. Within our classrooms and throughout our instructional day, we experience different social and emotional situations. Although the field of psychology still argues over how values are formed (Furth, 1990; Schwartz, 1999), they do agree that we establish our values contextually. Experiences are a part of that context.

Our values guide how we teach and, to some extent, who we teach. As educators, we make choices about how we are going to construct the learning environment. It is true that teachers who work to create accessible learning environments that focus on minimizing barriers and including every child in the process of education could be interpreted as good teachers. However, unless they are referencing the UDL framework to make those decisions, they are not implementing UDL.

MYTH: To do UDL, you have to use technology.

FALSE: An assumption that many make about UDL is that to "do" it, you have to use technology; this assumption is misleading. We cannot and should not ignore the impact technology has on us and on our students. Access to information, the ability to create, and the natural engagement that can come with technology can enrich a learning environment. It is, unfortunately true, that there are classrooms across the United States that still have limited access to technology, or the technology to which they have access is limited or outdated. To use this as an argument against UDL, however, is ill informed and an oversimplification of the affect teachers can have on learners. For centuries teachers have used the resources available to communicate ideas to students. UDL helps teachers look at available resources and potentially identify new ways to use them. As you learn more about UDL, you will likely identify examples and suggestions where the use of technology would improve or enhance a component within a lesson, but I urge you to collaborate with your peers to identify other no-tech or low-tech options that support your students' learning outcomes. And, again, shifting from *doing* UDL to *using* UDL as a decision-making framework gives us the strategy necessary to investigate all of the resources available.

CONCLUSION

This chapter provided definitions of terms related to UDL and replied to some common myths. You can see how, when fully applied, UDL has the potential to guide the use of the quality tools, resources, and strategies you have acquired and, subsequently, improve your students' learning experiences. The next section breaks down each of the principles along with their aligned guidelines and checkpoints.

Universal design for learning helps me take all of those good ideas I've learned over the years and organize them into lessons that I know will be successful, that my students will enjoy, and that lead to improved outcomes.

—Julie Calfee, English teacher, high school

II

THE PRINCIPLES OF UNIVERSAL DESIGN FOR LEARNING

> I know UDL works because the kids are engaged in what is going on, they're involved in the lesson, and they'll tell me if they understand or don't understand. To hear the kids say, "Oh, I've never gotten this before, and I understand it now," tells me that this works.
>
> —Allison White, math teacher, middle school

The three principles of Engagement, Representation, and Action and Expression create the overarching design of the UDL framework. They are the touch points when creating a learning environment. When Allison sees her students connecting with the lesson (Engagement) and she hears from their comments that they understand the material (Action and Expression), she knows she is giving it to them in an effective way (Representation).

As mentioned in Chapter 1, the three principles are based on the brain networks defined by CAST in their early work. Each principle directly correlates to how the brain responds within each of these learning phases. When the principles stand alone, they can feel almost vague, but the principles are purposefully defined broadly and there are interconnections between them. By giving them this level of breadth and cross connectedness, CAST has provided instructional choice to the teacher and a way to establish a general feel for the intended learning environment. Another way to think about the framework is to see it as something that helps you stand back and examine the big picture. It allows you to view your lesson and learning environment from 10,000 feet. Pretend that you are looking down on the land overlaid with the UDL framework. That framework gives you the chance to see how your lessons and learning environment come together to create a learning landscape.

Once you see how the principles are defined, the guidelines become the next level for understanding. The guidelines lead the selection of tools, resources, and strategies teachers use to design an accessible environment and develop lessons. The principles provide a global look and create that initial direction; the guidelines provide more specific guidance. Understanding the organization of the guidelines, though, is another important piece.

We want our students to know how to take the information they are given and gain meaning from it. We want them to be effective goal setters who know what steps to take to accomplish those goals. We want them to recognize themselves as learners who know how to facilitate their own learning. These are extremely important outcomes, which is why they are at the top of the matrix (Meyer, Rose, & Gordon, 2013).

What's Coming Up

The next three chapters begin with a brief section on the associated brain networks. This will help you answer that key question of *why* you are choosing the strategies you're choosing. Each chapter then continues with a description of the guidelines and checkpoints under that principle. I use analogies and scenarios to provide more description. Each description is based directly on information that can be found at the CAST web site (see http://www.udlcenter.org/aboutudl/udlguidelines).

Occasionally, the examples in this book touch on the Common Core State Standards. To date, 45 states have adopted the new Core Standards (National Governors Association Center for Best Practices and Council of Chief State School Officers, 2010). Because they are becoming a significant part of the teaching landscape, they are included within this book.

As described on their web site, the Common Core Standards are

- aligned with work and college expectations;

- are clear, understandable, and consistent;

- include rigorous content and application of knowledge through higher-order skills;

- build upon strengths and lessons of current state standards;

- are informed by other top performing counties, so that all students are prepared to succeed in our global economy and society; and

- are evidence-based. (Common Core State Standards Initiative, 2012)

According to the National Governors Association for Best Practices and the Council of Chief State School Officers (2010), the Common Core State Standards, as a whole, are written to guide teachers in what to teach but not how to teach it. The standards focus on the fundamentals of instruction, leaving curriculum designers and teachers to create content-rich lessons. The authors of these standards are also supportive of using appropriate supports to help students be successful.

The standards should also be read as allowing for the widest possible range of students to participate fully from the outset and as permitting appropriate accommodations to ensure maximum participation of students with special education needs. For example, for students with disabilities, reading should allow for the use of Braille, screen-reader technology, or other assistive devices, while writing should include the use of a scribe, computer, or speech-to-text technology. In a similar vein, speaking and listening should be interpreted broadly to include sign language (National Governors Association for Best Practices and the Council of Chief State School Officers, 2010, p. 6).

Requoting from the previous list, the intent that "the widest range of students [sic] participate fully from the outset" provides a pathway for the UDL framework.

I have listed the principles as they are portrayed on the UDL matrix from CAST with Engagement first, Representation second, and Action and Expression third (Meyer et al., 2013). The following chapters are also presented in that same order. The headers within the chapters are the same phrases used by CAST within their graphic organizer. In addition, there are icons in the margins to denote whether the header is for a guideline or a checkpoint. I also suggest you keep a marker at the graphic organizer page in Chapter 1.

A Few Cautions

This section is written as a guide. The environment design, lesson descriptions, and minilesson descriptions bring together a variety of guidelines and checkpoints. They represent the richness of the classroom. To help you learn about the specific guidelines and checkpoints, I will pull apart the examples and highlight the specific points within the examples. There is a danger to this, however.

Although I touch on the checkpoints under each of the guidelines, the chapters cannot include a comprehensive set of examples. It would make the book impossibly long. UDL is dynamic, far-reaching, and structured to bring together quality, research-based, and evidence-based practices. There are a multitude of potential examples and scenarios for the wide variety of learning environments and the variable learners within those environments. By offering the chosen scenarios and analogies in this book, I run the risk of narrowing UDL. The framework is dense with choice because it is grounded in a broad array of research, so it will be your task to transfer what you learn from these examples to the tools, resources, and strategies you use in your setting. Remember to ask the key question, "*Why* am I choosing this tool, resource, or strategy?" and "What purpose will it serve within the framework?"

My second caution is to allow some distance from the information. The checkpoints across and within the guidelines can seem similar to one another in definition and intent. If you spend time trying to see the difference, it can become overwhelming. I suggest thinking about each guideline as a piece of the puzzle. The checkpoints merely shape the puzzle piece. Ultimately, the guidelines all fit together to create the UDL framework.

The specifics are within this book's examples, but I encourage you to move between the specific examples and the generalizations. As I stated previously, to get too involved in the specifics might lead you to being overwhelmed. UDL is rich, diverse, and deep. I suggest you see this as an opportunity to connect the great tools, resources, and strategies you already use to a framework that will help you design an even stronger learning environment and lessons. Another way to enhance your understanding is to visit the National Center on UDL, where they break down the checkpoints and offer some curricular examples (http://www.udlcenter.org/implementation/examples).

A third caution is technology. The use of technology can enhance all of the principles, but you should never assume that the technology is automatically addressing the UDL framework. Better stated, I never assume that a piece of technology (e.g., hardware, software) is being used in a UDL way. This connects to the myth in Chapter 2: If you purchase a UDL product, then you're doing UDL. Behind the use of any tool, resource, or strategy must be intentional use. *Why* you're using the technology, be it a calculator, a tablet, or a writing program, determines whether you are implementing UDL. Ultimately, your job is to remain inquisitive and purposeful about the development of your learning environment and lessons. The framework simply guides you when deciding what questions to ask.

The following chapters are dense with information. You may choose to read them straight through, use them as a reference, or hop around. Read them in a way that fits your needs so that you can come to understand the UDL framework. As mentioned in Chapter 1, under the heading Designing, we are not instructed to use every checkpoint or a certain number of guidelines within each lesson. Instead, I suggest exploring the guidelines and checkpoints and reflect on what you are already doing. Then ask how what you are doing directly relates back to the framework. Next, investigate how you can bring those and other checkpoints and guidelines to life within the structure of your learning environment with the goal of lessening any structural or instructional barriers. By addressing barriers within the environment first, the design and implementation of your lessons will flow more easily.

3

ENGAGEMENT

To me, the key element is always student engagement.
—Elizabeth Bays, world language teacher of Japanese, high school

We know that when a student comes into a learning environment, that student's brain needs to be turned on or engaged. This allows for learning to begin (Rose & Meyer, 2002). That does not mean the teacher can check off engagement for the lesson. Engagement lasts throughout the lesson. It overlaps with the principles of Representation and Action and Expression. How so? Because while you are representing the information you want your students to learn, you need to be sure they are still involved in the lesson. When they are actively expressing their knowledge, they need to still feel emotionally connected to the information (Storbeck & Clore, 2012).

THE AFFECTIVE NETWORKS

The affective networks allow us to engage in learning. These paths enable us to evaluate patterns and connect an emotional significance to them (Rose & Meyer, 2002). Patterns relate to the information that comes to us through our senses. How we relate to that information is filtered through our memories, needs, and emotions. Although there are generalizations that can be made about emotional responses (e.g., showing happiness when experiencing something desirable), because we are individuals, the experience making us happy will vary from person to person (Rose & Meyer, 2002). This has direct implications for the classroom.

If you and I were to listen to a poem at the same time, you might be enthralled by the language and with the images it creates in your mind. You are connected to the lesson and eager to learn more. Meanwhile, I am bored and uninterested. The words mean nothing to me, I've decided poems are dumb, and I am now thinking about something else to occupy my time. How you and I respond to the poem and hearing the poem reflects the results of our affective networks. The good news is that our teacher can help connect me to the poem and the experience of poetry through the principle of Engagement.

THE PRINCIPLE, GUIDELINES, AND CHECKPOINTS

The principle of Engagement is structured around three guidelines (see Figure 3.1).

- Offering options for self-regulation—students gaining skills in self-monitoring to gauge their behaviors and their learning and take charge of their own learning (Meyer, Rose & Gordon, 2013).

- Sustaining effort and persistence—providing opportunities where students naturally work with their peers, focus on the task at hand, and receive directive and supportive feedback from the instructor.

- Recruiting interest—gaining student interest by tapping in to who they are and to their interests.

Provide Options for Self-Regulation

This guideline suggests opportunities for students to demonstrate their highest level of independence. Under Engagement, that means that the students recognize themselves as learners and how to facilitate their own learning. The following checkpoints will help you design an environment that moves students toward such an achievement.

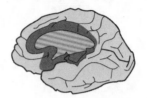

Provide Multiple Means of
Engagement
Purposeful, motivated learners

Provide options for self-regulation
+ Promote expectations and beliefs that optimize motivation
+ Facilitate personal coping skills and strategies
+ Develop self-assessment and reflection

Provide options for sustaining effort and persistence
+ Heighten salience of goals and objectives
+ Vary demands and resources to optimize challenge
+ Foster collaboration and community
+ Increase mastery-oriented feedback

Provide options for recruiting interest
+ Optimize individual choice and autonomy
+ Optimize relevance, value, and authenticity
+ Minimize threats and distractions

Figure 3.1. CAST's principle of Engagement.
From Meyer, A., Rose, D.H., & Gordon, D.T. [2013]. *Universal design for learning theory and practice.* Wakefield, MA: National Center on Universal Design for Learning; adapted by permission.

SELF-REGULATION SKILLS IN HIGH SCHOOL: JULIE CALFEE AND STUDENT TASK MANAGEMENT Julie Calfee, a high school English teacher, knows the hard work of nurturing students' self-regulation. Many of her students come from environments in which they haven't been provided opportunities or guided toward self-regulated behaviors. Julie realizes that she has to remove judgment and let her students begin where they are. In the case of homework, that might mean some students only complete 2 of the 15 questions on the homework assignment. Instead of judging them for their incomplete work, she recognizes that these students are learning how to set aside time for homework, a task they typically find insurmountable. She doesn't stop there, though. Julie uses the UDL framework to help her design lessons and environments that support her students as they determine a starting point for self-regulation. She then builds on that level of accomplishment through setting higher and higher expectations.

Promote Expectations and Beliefs That Optimize Motivation

When you establish and make obvious the expectations of the learning environment, students are more likely to successfully achieve those expectations (Colvin, Sugai, & Kameenui, 1994; Lewis & Sugai, 1999; Lewis, Sugai, & Colvin, 1998). Making them obvious, though, means specific and direct instruction (Lewis & Sugai, 1999). CAST suggests checklists, guides, prompts, reminders, and rubrics, but students also benefit from modeling.

Specific to this checkpoint is assisting the students' development of self-regulated, on-task behaviors (e.g., the ability to ignore distractions) and the ability to self-monitor and self-reflect on their responses to distractions. Students can begin working on these skills at a very young age.

Bodrova, Leong, and Akhutina (2011) dug back into the original research on self-regulation in early childhood by Vygotsky (whose research is at the base of UDL) and Luria. That work created the basis for their own research. They found that regulation skills emerge through social interactions, participation in what they termed other-regulation (where they experience being regulated by others and by regulating the behaviors of others), recognizing shared behaviors, the use of private talk (learning to self-mediate after being guided in mediation), and using external objects to remind them of appropriate behaviors. No matter the age, most students need structures to help them achieve in this area. Tools from self-monitoring sheets to personal conversations will promote the desired outcomes.

Self-monitoring tools should be student specific, though they might be framed by the overall classroom expectations. If your students have decided and agreed upon specific expectations (e.g., the overarching phrase for your middle school classroom is: "Be on time, bring your stuff, be polite, and be nice"), then each student's sheet would have these expectations listed. However, additional expectations might be added depending on the skill focus. If students are working on a collaborative project, there might be a location for them to self-assess how they used their time (the majority of the time, I was: on-task, distracted, off-task). They can do a check-in with their peers to find out if they agree with each other's assessment and how to improve if needed. All of this requires you to foster a trusting, open, and task-oriented environment that supports these types of interactions.

The other part of this checkpoint is goal setting. Helping students set realistic goals is the first step. Next comes helping them determine what steps they need to take to achieve those goals, and then comes the step discussed throughout this book—self-reflection (Cooper, Horn, & Strahan, 2005; Zimmerman, Bonner, & Kovach, 1996). They will need support in these steps and maintaining a focus on their goals. Students, just like us, can modify their goals. Learning that level of flexibility is equally as important to the achievement of the goal.

Facilitate Personal Coping Skills and Strategies

We all have coping skills, and some of those skills we use aren't appropriate for some settings. You've likely figured out how to gauge your own frustrations, anger, phobias, or other situations that might cause you to act in a non–socially appropriate way. Our students don't come with the maturity and experience we have, so we need to model the skill set and provide them with mastery feedback and other supports to help them build on their skills.

Underlying the supports you offer is the interpersonal relationship you have with your students. Research tells us that the interpersonal relationships students build while in school are an important factor in their success (Black, 2002; Hamre & Pianta, 2001; Whitted, 2011). These relationships can help or hinder their school connectedness, an indicator for developing strong coping skills and strategies.

In a study that specifically looked at the coping skills of elementary school students related to school connectedness, researchers found that students with higher levels of school connectedness showed lower levels of outward anger and stress and higher levels of social connectedness (Rice, Kang, Weaver, & Howell, 2008). Another study with middle school students showed that students who exemplified anger-reflection/control had better peer relationships (Thomas & Smith, 2004).

Coping skills don't magically appear when school connectedness occurs, though. You will need to purposefully demonstrate these skills to some students, whereas others will pick up on them naturally. When you see a student who is not responding to a student in a developmentally appropriate way, you can provide direct instruction through personal conversation, supportive suggestions, and by offering praise when the student adopts a new and appropriate coping skill.

SUSTAINING THE INTEREST OF SHY STUDENTS: JULIE CALFEE AND STUDENT COPING SKILLS In some cases, coping skills and strategies might need to be offered to students who aren't naturally outgoing. Consider a shy high school student who is operating within an environment designed to encourage student-led discussion or student performance. Julie Calfee promotes coping skills and strategies by pairing shy students with outgoing students, providing both students with the opportunity to shine. For example, the outgoing student is given the role of acting out the scene while the shy student sits to the side and reads the text out loud. An outgoing person herself, Julie spends time identifying and structuring specific activities and supports that ensure the participation of her students who are shy or reluctant speakers.

Develop Self-Assessment and Reflection

The importance of self-reflection by students has been studied since Dewey (Williams, 2006). Researchers then continued to look at the role of reflection, expanding its definition and importance. Some researchers built on the work of George Herbert Mead and Lev Vygotsky to define self-reflection as a sociocultural phenomenon (Cinnamond & Zimpher, 1990). Those researchers found that when individuals were interacting with the environment, they constructed a sense of self through self-reflection (Williams, 2006). Next, researchers studied the connection between self-reflection and self-regulation (Bandura, 1986; Zimmerman & Bandura, 1994). Both were found to be significantly linked to academic performance (Bandura, 1993; Pajares, 1996; Pajares & Johnson, 1994). Interestingly, learning through self-reflection has been demonstrated as a self-conscious process. It can become automatic, but only after specific practice. Children younger than 7 years are least likely to automatically self-reflect due to their developmental stage (Valkanova, 2004; Yussen, 1985; Zelazo, 2000). Ultimately, self-reflection is a learned process and one that can lead to improving academic performance (Williams, 2006). Any practice that requires your students to stop and consider what they have learned or produced touches on self-reflection and self-assessment.

Because the concept of self-assessment and reflection is inherently that of one's self in relation to an environment, having students consider who they are as a learner becomes a focus. Questions such as the following help students gain self-reflective skills:

- I prefer to work by myself when . . .

- I enjoy working with others when . . .

- When I don't understand something, I . . .

- When I have to get something read, I . . .

- When the environment I'm in is too noisy for me, I . . .

- When I'm distracted and not getting my assignment done, I . . .

Self-assessment and reflection can be contextualized by the activities of the classroom, too. For example, the upcoming Common Core State Standards (CCSS) place a strong emphasis on writing, specifically bringing to light the three areas of research, *reflection*, and revision (Calkins, Ehrenworth, & Lehman, 2012). Because students will be expected to write daily across all content areas this offers an automatic platform, but you will still need to provide guidance. This can come through verbal prompts, rubrics, paired work with conversational prompts, and full class reflections. Creating an environment with consistent prompts around self-assessment and reflection can assist your students in their adoption of these skills.

Some of your prompts will be overarching and some will be specific. Specific prompts can attend to the typical requirements linked to classroom work (e.g., Did you put your name on your paper?), while others will be assignment specific. For example, if your students are working on using their vocabulary words in sentences, giving them the following prompts can help them review their work prior to handing it in.

- Make sure you can locate all of your vocabulary words in your writing assignment.

- How can you tell if you have demonstrated the definition of those words?

- How will you change your sentence to show your understanding of the word?

- Choose your favorite sentence and share it with your partner. Listen to your partner's feedback.

Self-assessment and reflection are also vital in connection to behaviors. Giving students the opportunity to reflect on how they handled positive or challenging situations can help them build an understanding of their own relationship with the environment. By helping them identify positive behavioral outcomes, they begin to understand what behaviors are appropriate in a specific environment.

Providing Options for Sustaining Effort and Persistence

This guideline focuses on providing opportunities for students to connect with the goal of the lesson, naturally work with their peers, focus on the current task, and receive direct and supportive feedback from the instructor. When students learn how to sustain their efforts and discover ways to develop persistence, they gain even more ownership of their learning.

Heighten Salience of Goals and Objectives

We all want our students to work toward the goal and objectives of the lesson. In Chapter 6, I will discuss the construct of the goal and how students should know and understand the goal of the lesson. This checkpoint adds a little flavor to the concept of goals and objectives.

When something is salient it stands out. It is so conspicuous that it almost jumps out at you. Although only the most creative will decide to make their goals and objectives jump up or down, there is hope for the rest of us. Let's look at saliency as it relates to other classroom activities.

You might have your classroom set up to guide your students toward independence—another underlying and desired outcome of UDL. To get your students to follow through on these actions, you had to raise the salience of those activities. In each of those cases, you've figured out ways to make those actions more salient. In Table 3.1 I have listed a few common classroom management objectives seen at the elementary, middle, and high school levels. Under those are ways to make those objectives more salient. I have gone a bit further and listed some ways you might scaffold the experience so those learners who aren't initially successful, or who will always need support, can become a part of the successful classroom culture.

Things don't change much when it comes to the salience of your goals. I suggest posting the goal. Writing the goal in the same place each day is a first step. That kind of consistency is satisfying and helpful to your students, but they will need more support than this, and you get to decide how you will offer that. Maybe you will read the goal aloud to them. Maybe you create the role of "goal reader" as one of your classroom jobs. That student points to the goal and reads it aloud to the class each day during that job's rotation. Maybe you require that your students enter the goal into their physical or digital assignment notebook or sheet each day.

Table 3.1. Scaffolding examples

Objective: Elementary—When students return from recess, they hang up their coats.

Salience: Students practice this action and receive praise and specific feedback (i.e., "Thank you for hanging up your coat, Ji Yeon"). Maybe some of your students need buddies to remind them to hang up their coats versus throw them on the floor when they come in from the playground.

Objective: Middle school—Students put their homework in a specific basket.

Salience: Students are verbally reminded to place their homework in the basket during the first few weeks of school. If students repeatedly forget to do this, talk with them individually to find out how they'd like to be reminded. Do they want a buddy to remind them? Do they need a reminder at their desk? Do they need a code word that triggers their memory?

Objective: High school—Students write down the assignment for the night in their assignment book.

Salience: The assignment is written on a section of your board highlighted by brightly colored tape, chalk, or marker to draw their attention to that area. Begin each class reminding the students to write down their assignment or otherwise note it (e.g., record it into their phone, type it into their calendar, have a scribe enter it into their notebook). Use cooperative learning to your advantage by allowing students to check in on each other's understanding of the proposed assignment.

(Note that I said "enter." This allows the student to use the means that fits their needs best, e.g., writing it, dictating it, typing it.) For more information about goals, see Chapter 7.

Vary Demands and Resources to Optimize Challenge

 This checkpoint focuses on the concept of scaffolding. Scaffolding refers to the steps you take to help students learn a task or skill. Scaffolding is dynamic, changing over time. Typically used temporarily, scaffolding should remain in place only until the student can successfully accomplish the task or skill independent of the scaffold. The hope is that the support is lessened until the student achieves independence. The examples I gave in Table 3.1 all have scaffolds. In the case of the elementary students, one suggested scaffold was the coat-hanging buddy.

For example, you have a student named Nicole who never remembers to hang up her coat. She always has to leave the reading circle to hang it up, which frustrates her because she loses her seat. We all know how important seating is on the reading carpet. You know that her best friend, Chandra, regularly hangs up her coat.

We'll assume you have talked to Nicole to see if she has a reason for not hanging up her coat, a crucial first step. It appears that she doesn't do it because she's so excited to grab her place on the reading carpet. You let Nicole know that you want to help her remember to hang up her coat so she can stay on the reading carpet. Would she like a buddy to help her remember, so she doesn't have to go back and hang it up each day? She says yes. You talk with Chandra to see if she's willing to gently remind her friend to hang up her coat. You give Chandra specific examples of what "gentle" means by modeling polite, positive, and quiet reminder phrases.

After a few weeks of daily reminders and successful coat hanging, you ask Nicole if she still needs reminders every day or if she's ready for occasional reminders. She replies that she's ready for occasional reminders, so you tell Chandra to skip reminding Nicole the next day. If Nicole has an unsuccessful day, assure her that this is okay. She still has to hang up her coat, and Chandra will remind her again the next day. Repeat this cycle until Chandra is reminding Nicole less and less. The hope is that Nicole will eventually reach the point where she independently remembers to hang up her coat.

TRANSFER AND GENERALIZATION: JULIE CALFEE AND STUDENT ENGAGEMENT   One way Julie Calfee scaffolds her high school English lessons is to use graphic organizers. She uses them to structure her students' learning both in class and when they are doing their homework. Because her students receive guided practice during class on how to use the graphic organizers, they are able to organize their thoughts using that same format at home. Her desire is to provide the students with enough consistency and patterns in learning that they can transfer those skills from environment to environment and from assignment to assignment.

The previous example of scaffolding leaned toward an example of demands. When you think about scaffolding resources, you're considering how to scaffold a single resource or how to use other resources to help the student move toward the desired outcome. Resources are the items students use to learn information. Ranging from books to digital options, some resources are predisposed to natural scaffolding. Something as static as a book must be partnered with something else to provide scaffolding. Proven methods for scaffolding text-based copies, outside of rewriting or recording it, include using a ruler or folded piece of paper placed under the line being read to guide the eyes and slow the student's reading (Ruffin, 2012), clear report covers (colored sheet of plastic) laid across the page to enhance their attention and address certain reading disabilities (Harris & MacRow-Hill, 1999; Noble, Orton, Irlen, & Robinson, 2004; Robinson & Conway, 2000; Ruffin, 2012; Solan, Ficarra, Brannan, & Rucker, 1998), and paired reading to give full auditory access to the information (Fuchs, Fuchs, & Burish, 2000; Koskinen & Blum, 1986; Strickland, Ganske, & Monroe, 2002). If one or more of the strategies are successful, students can adopt them. As the students become more practiced with these scaffolds, you give them the opportunity to graduate beyond them.

Digital resources provide a plethora of scaffolding options, some of them built into everyday software. Personal computers using the operating system Microsoft Vista and earlier versions have a range of supports for individuals who have low or no vision, challenges in using their hands or arms, and intellectual or cognitive disabilities (Microsoft, 2012). Users can access their computer's control panel and select the "ease of access center" to peruse these options and see if what is offered benefits them. Apple products also have a built-in range of supports that are discussed within their "Apple in Education" section of their web site (Apple, 2012). Although these digital offerings are specifically identified as supports for individuals with disabilities, they can be useful to all students.

As described at the beginning of this book, if you've walked along a sidewalk pulling a wheeled briefcase, a suitcase, or pushing a stroller, you have likely used the curb cuts. Designed to benefit individuals using wheelchairs, curb cuts are ubiquitous in the United States and are expected. You get where you're going more efficiently because you can use the curb cut. Digital supports can be synonymous with curb cuts when they are selected thoughtfully. They may be used permanently by some students, and temporarily by others. In those instances, they could be a part of your scaffolded design.

There are thousands of other digital resources, from handheld gaming systems to digital tablets to classroom-specific devices (e.g., digital whiteboard touch screens, handheld voting systems). Each will have settings and options within their operating systems that can help you scaffold the resource. Scaffolding can always include interpersonal supports from a peer or an adult. Some students simply need a partner to help them learn the technology or get through the activity, game, or online lesson the first few times. Once the student gains an understanding of how the device and/or software works, they can be given the opportunity to become more independent.

Foster Collaboration and Community

Just as the previous examples demonstrate, interpersonal relationships are extremely important to learning. In fact, the current postsecondary professional world requires students to be effective communicators and collaborators. The new CCSS have standards for speaking and listening. For these areas there are six anchor standards that are organized in two groups: Comprehension and Collaboration, and Presentation of Knowledge and Ideas. Comprehension and Collaboration centers on students gaining an understanding through working together. Presentation of Knowledge and Ideas centers on student-led oral presentations (Calkins et al., 2012). Both UDL and the new CCSS want you to create an environment that supports collaboration. Knowing that cooperative learning leads to stronger collaborative skills (Baloche, 1998), why is cooperative learning such an important skill to practice in the classroom?

Haydon, Maheady, and Hunter (2010) looked closely at the cooperative learning literature by Johnson and Johnson (1999), Johnson, Johnson, and Holubec (1991), and Putnam (1998) and gathered the four essential skills that enhance students' experiences:

1. Positive interdependence; all group members are concerned about each other's performance toward achieving the group goal.

2. Individual accountability; each student is responsible for learning academic content and contributing to the group.

3. Face to face positive interaction; while working, students directly interact with one another.

4. Group processing; students evaluate whether group goals were achieved and whether there was an equal opportunity for responding. (Haydon et al., 2010, pp. 223–224)

Fortunately, there are scores of useful resources available online and in books and articles for teachers to use when designing collaborative activities. The University of Minnesota's Collaborative Learning Center has an in-depth web site that provides both theoretical and concrete, how-to information. It is an excellent starting point for exploring collaboration and cooperative learning.

COLLABORATION AND COMMUNITY: JULIE CALFEE AND SCAFFOLD-ING Julie Calfee uses scaffolding to support all of her high school students through particularly difficult passages of *Romeo and Juliet*. She recognizes that without the scaffolding, some of her students will not be persistent and gain an understanding of the text. She finds that by getting students up, moving, and thinking about strategic phrases, they are more likely to connect to the text. By giving the students specific, workable segments of the play, she builds on their current knowledge and learning preferences. This improves their ability to collaborate with their peers. Her expectations, though, have not been altered and neither have her connections to the standards. Students are still expected to identify and articulate their understanding of personification, imagery and poetic terms. They can do this because Julie has built on their engagement with the difficult text to help them reach new levels of persistence.

Increase Mastery-Oriented Feedback

As teachers, we provide feedback to our students by writing on their homework, offering verbal feedback, looking at them askance when they aren't on task, and rewarding them for positive behaviors. All of this is feedback, but this checkpoint is addressing the feedback we offer to students to increase their learning. Mastery feedback provides specific direction to the student. Putting an X next to a problem only tells the student one thing: the student did not correctly answer the problem. Although writing "good" next to a sentence on a student's paper might make the student feel good, it does not provide specific information about the sentence. Both examples have limited the student's potential for learning.

When you provide mastery feedback, you are giving the student a clear pathway to take toward a positive outcome. Feedback can be directive (e.g., "Remember that *it's* is a contraction. You wanted to use *its* as a possessive noun."), or it can be posed as a question (e.g., "Do you want to use the contraction *it is* here, should this be a possessive noun?"). Both provide feedback, but you would determine which kind to use based on the needs of the student. You might also decide to provide overall feedback. If so, make sure it is specific enough for the student to make the changes you are requesting.

Beyond what I have written previously, you might still ask, "Why provide mastery feedback?" Just as you are more successful when you reflect on your teaching practice and then make adjustments, we need to support our students in becoming reflective learners so they too can make changes to their work (Chappuis & Stiggins, 2002). This means that you should make the process of mastery feedback move full circle. Check your students' understanding of the feedback. Did they understand it? Can they now apply it to similar problems or situations? Do they need additional support? This cycle will naturally occur in your classroom through the process of formative assessments (discussed more in Chapter 5).

Options for Recruiting Interest

When we think about recruiting the interest of our students, we can get stuck on the aspect of entertainment, but recruiting interest has more depth to it than simple entertainment. This is exemplified by the first checkpoint.

Optimizing Choice and Autonomy

Giving students a choice does not mean leaving everything open ended or that students will always choose the assignment that is easiest for them to accomplish. I suggest that teachers consider structured choice. When teachers design the environment to include choice and to combine choice with structure (versus unguided or unregulated choice), students are more engaged in the lesson (Jang, Reeve, & Deci, 2010). You can incorporate student choice in areas ranging from classroom management (e.g., they choose where to read during silent reading, the types of rewards they receive for positive behaviors, their choice of learning strategies or platforms) to academics (e.g., they choose which method they will use to solve math problems, they can complete sections of their work in whatever order they choose, they choose how they will gather information). Anything that expands student choice fits here. When students operate within an environment designed with structured choice, they sense a bit of freedom, but at the same time they can be guided to understand how their choices affect them. This reflects autonomy, another piece of the first checkpoint under recruiting interest.

When students are autonomous, they are self-governed. Being autonomous does little for learning, however, unless students know how to apply that autonomy. This touches on creating an environment that supports self-determination, a theory furthered by Richard Ryan and Edward Deci (2000; Deci & Ryan, 2002). One component of this expansive theory states that teachers who support self-determination guide students' personal autonomy by seeing the lesson from the students' perspective.

> I think about when I was in high school. Because if I wouldn't have wanted to do it then why would they want to do it now?
>
> —Elizabeth Bays, world language teacher of Japanese, high school

Additionally, they identify and cultivate the students' needs, interests, and preferences and provide challenges appropriate for the student. They do all of this by "highlighting meaningful learning goals; and presenting interesting, relevant and enriched activities" (Jang et al., 2010, p. 589). That sounds a lot like UDL, doesn't it? These underlying pieces of self-determination are definitely an important piece.

A strategy that is commonly associated with UDL and demonstrates choice and autonomy is a strategy called Tic-Tac-Toe (Edyburn, 2009, 2011). Using a single sheet of paper, the teacher draws a Tic-Tac-Toe grid into which nine different activities are written. Students can then choose three activities by drawing a line across, down, or diagonally. Teachers design the nine activities so that each allows students to demonstrate different strengths and skills. A tic-tac-toe grid created by two teachers in Bartholomew Consolidated School Corporation in 2009 was selected by Microsoft's U.S. Innovation Teachers Forum, taking top honors. By reading through the Tic-Tac-Toe example in Figure 3.2, you can see the variety of choice and the autonomy the students were offered.

You can also watch a video of these two teachers created by Carrie Hipsher and posted at http://vimeo.com/6104437 (Hipsher, 2009). The guideline, Provide Options for Physical Action, under the principle of Action and Expression is also naturally embedded within the tic-tac-toe strategy. I will return to this strategy under that principle.

Industrial revolution
Project Guide: 9th grade
Directions: Select three project options to complete. You may select three across, three down or three through the middle.

Photo-essay/art	Research/writing	Musical
Find pictures (or create your own) of working conditions during the industrial revolution age (1800s) and photos from our current time. Photos can show child labor, factories, housing, etc. Put them together in a collage using multimedia. Examples might be a PowerPoint, an online photo album on a site like Snapfish, a web site, scrapbook, and so forth. Minimum of 20 pictures. Include captions with your pictures to provide a description of the images.	Research current child labor laws in the U.S. Find out what the laws are and then consider: Should there be stiffer legislation? Should there be more careful monitoring of children's work by parent and teacher? What should the rules be regarding work hours and responsibilities? Should there be rules regarding interference with school work? Punishments for violators? Write a letter to a policy maker or editor expressing your opinions, based on your research.	Create a soundtrack of at least ten songs that shows the working and living conditions during the industrial revolution and/or songs about working and living conditions today. Themes you might include are sickness, stress, low pay, pollution, and so forth. Design the cover of the CD as well as give an explanation of why you selected those songs.
Drama	**Economics/technical**	**Logical/sequential**
Write and produce a movie based on the life of someone living during the industrial revolution. The person can be a member of the working poor, a wealthy capitalist, a middle class individual, a child laborer, etc. You can act out the movie or use software to produce it.	Working conditions still vary widely depending on the work being performed and the area in which the work is located. Research global companies that have a good reputation for high quality working conditions. Create a top ten list of modern companies. Define your criteria and defend your list. Then, create a recruitment advertisement for one of the companies. Ex: commercial, poster, web site	Create a series of charts that show rapid urban growth during the industrial revolution. Include information on population, productivity, average life span, pollution information, and so forth. For example, use locations such as Manchester or London, England, and Lowell, Massachusetts. Create the same series of charts that show rapid urban growth for modern times. Ex: China, India, and so forth.
Science/health	**Technical**	**Creative writing**
Poor and crowded living conditions during the Industrial Revolution led to the spread of many illnesses, including cholera. Research the causes, symptoms, and treatments for cholera. Then, create a public service campaign to educate the masses about the illness. This can include posters, brochures, commercials, and so forth.	Many inventions were created during the Industrial Revolution. These include the seed drill, the spinning jenny, cotton gin, steam engines, telephone, sewing machine, Morse Code (electrical signals over a telegraph), railroad, among many others. Select three and create instructional/user manuals for the inventions. The manuals can be hand created or computer generated using software such as Publisher.	Imagine that you are living during the early years of the Industrial Revolution. Choose to be one of the following: a factory worker, a child laborer, or a working class mother. Write a series of diary entries (at least five) in the role of your assumed character. Be sure to record the events of your day and include specific details about your life. You should include not only activities and observations, but also your feelings and emotions.

Figure 3.2. A teacher's tic-tac-toe lesson.
From Streeval, A., & Armstrong, H.A. [2009]. *Industrial revolution project guide: Grade 9*. Reprinted by permission of Autumne Streeval, M.S., & Harriet A. Armstrong, M.S., CFCS.

Optimize Relevance, Value, and Authenticity

Another checkpoint under the guideline of recruiting interest involves offering relevance, value, and authenticity. This can be done by connecting your lesson to students' current experiences.

RELEVANCE, VALUE, AND AUTHENTICITY: JULIE CALFEE AND SHAKESPEARE Julie Calfee's first step toward building relevance, value, and authenticity for her high school students is to put herself in her students' shoes. For example, when reading Romeo and Juliet the challenge most readers face is keeping the two families straight. She uses the colors blue and red to represent the two families. These also happen to be the color schemes utilized in other movie renditions which she uses as examples. She also connects the story to gang culture with which the students are familiar from television, videos and from some of their own experiences. Through these two strategies she makes the story familiar and personal with the purpose of raising the level of authenticity.

Consider this scenario: A high school physics lesson is focused on introducing conduction (heat transfer). The goal of the lesson is to explore the meaning of conduction and to identify hypotheses. To represent the process of conduction, the teacher is prepared to show a 2-minute video, follow up with a student-led experiment, and end with a closing discussion. To provide more opportunities for her students to engage in the lesson, the teacher begins by taking a poll on the number of students who drink coffee, hot chocolate, hot tea, or to list other hot beverages. She's sure to take feedback from students who don't like to drink hot beverages. The teacher then asks how many of them like to warm their hands around that ceramic mug that holds the hot liquid. She asks, "Why does that ceramic mug get hot?" She creates a quick two-column table with the words *Know* and *Need to Know* written at the top. The teacher writes down what the students know and don't know about the question within the appropriate columns. To move them toward the topic of conduction, the teacher uses a few additional guiding prompts, such as, "What is making the ceramic mug hot?" "If you leave that hot liquid in the ceramic mug, what eventually happens to the liquid?" "Does what happened to the liquid have anything to do with energy?" The Know and Need to Know list becomes the undercarriage of that lesson on conduction. This 5-minute exercise can help students connect an everyday or regular experience with the overall topic of heat conduction.

This example focuses on relevance, value, and authenticity in a variety of ways. Although some students might not enjoy drinking hot liquids, it is likely they have held one. Because this is an introductory conversation, you have the opportunity to offer that experience later during class to connect those students who don't remember the sensation. The value in this lesson is fairly easy; it has to do with drinking something. It is an activity that most experience. Finally, the authenticity lies in the knowledge that hot liquids are experienced across most cultures.

Minimize Threats and Distractions

The last checkpoint under this guideline talks about minimizing threats and distractions. When a student feels threatened within an environment, that student will not function well. What does threatened mean? Outside of the literal meaning, which could be associated with bullying, feeling threatened can coincide with feeling insignificant, uninformed, or inadequate.

Scenario: Tanya teaches in an urban district that faces budget cuts each year, yet class size seems to grow. There isn't much access to technology. Three separate carts with 4-year-old desktops on them can be signed out from the library, and there is a Smartboard in the computer lab that also has 25 stationary desktops. She doesn't have access to any field-trip dollars this year, but she can bring in people to speak.

Her students are working on a natural sciences unit where they are identifying the anatomy of a species of fish. They will also talk about the habitat of these fish and how that habitat affects the life of the fish. Because she can't take the students to the fish, she's hoping she can bring the fish to them. She decides on two strategies. First, she signs out two of the computers and finds a conservancy web site with some online instructional games that will let her students see the habitat and fish on the screen. Setting them up as stations, the students all have an opportunity to use the computers. Second, she contacts that same local conservancy and finds out that they can send a speaker with examples (e.g., water samples, plant samples, samples of fish).

Tanya is familiar with UDL and has been using the framework to make decisions about her classroom and lessons. She knows that her students will be very curious and interested in the speaker and the examples, and it could be an easy thing to say that she covered the principle of Engagement with this simple invitation. However, she knows better. Under the bottom guideline of Engagement, she's learned to think about potential threats or distractions.

Several of her students don't react well to strangers. Some of them have experienced situations where strangers equaled danger, while others become overly excited and might not act appropriately. Still others will be overstimulated by a visitor with examples, and they won't be able to pay attention. This last dynamic keeps some of her fellow teachers from inviting guests. Other students are so self-conscious about their knowledge that they are unwilling to participate in group discussions for fear that they will say something wrong. Tanya knows that these students will sometimes turn to acting out rather than risk the possibility of being embarrassed by their lack of knowledge. All of these behaviors ranging from inattention to outbursts can derail a lesson or her entire classroom.

Fortunately, Tanya has learned to look for resources that help her implement the different guidelines of UDL, specifically the guideline of options for recruiting interest. She has learned techniques for setting behavioral expectations with the students, giving them time to practice those expectations, and how to appropriately reward the students for their attentiveness. Although she already has supports in place within her learning environment, she must still think through the framework each day. Tanya continues to affect the learning environment she has created, even when she's not the primary facilitator of learning.

This example uses "threat" in several ways. One is an emotion that links to danger. The other is an emotion that links to insecurities about learning. A threatening environment is one where the student is not comfortable or confident in participating. We lose our ability to concentrate when we feel threatened. Distraction is another piece to this guideline.

We know that students can be distracted for a variety of reasons. When creating your environment, consider the distractions you can minimize by thinking about the five senses. For example, you can establish flexible seating in your classroom so you can move students to areas that meet their needs. The needs that might include seeing the information (sight), hearing over the noisy heating vent (hearing), receiving your gentle touch on the shoulder to return to the task (touch). Outside of the five senses, there are other ways you can minimize threats. Keeping a calendar of events so students know when visitors are coming is one example and establishing specific routines is another.

CONCLUSION

This chapter has provided an overview of the affective networks to provide a basis for the principle of Engagement. Next, examples and analogies brought Engagement to life. Much more than a quest to keep the attention of students, UDL's Engagement delves into our brain's needs. When you create a learning environment where each student feels respected and academically safe, they are more likely to take risks in learning. When we use the principle of Engagement to design our learning environment, our students have more opportunities to connect with that environment and the lessons within it.

Revisiting Anthony's Lesson

Anthony's lesson was about adding integers. Because this was the first day of the topic, he found a short cartoon video in which the characters were numbers and talked through what it meant to be an integer. It showed them sitting on a number line and then how they combined through addition. He gave each student a number line to use and to keep in his or her folder and then followed up with a worksheet. Students worked independently, and he went to their desks if they had questions.

This sounds like a UDL lesson, doesn't it? Anthony had a cartoon video, so the students must have been engaged. Add that to the number lines at their desks which they used, and he must have been representing the information to them. Then, they worked on a worksheet. That's expression, right? This must be a UDL lesson!

Let's interview Anthony about this lesson.

Loui: "Hi Anthony. Thanks for answering some questions about your lesson."

Anthony: "Sure thing!"

(continued)

(*continued*)

Loui: "I'm curious why you chose that video."

Anthony: "We all know kids love the cartoon videos, and I thought the cartoon did a great job of introducing integers."

Loui: "It did look like they enjoyed it. Now, you followed that up with some additional instruction, and then the students worked on their worksheets. Can you tell me why you chose those activities?"

Anthony: "Well, I always follow a video with some lecture. Otherwise, I'm not teaching, right? The students have to hear and see me teach or else I'm not doing my job. Then, I wanted to see if they were getting it, so I gave them the worksheets. I needed some more scores for the grade book, and those need to be individual scores. This way, I can show where they started and then how much growth they have achieved in the next two days as we work on integers. I can't get those scores from group work because that's not fair to all of the students."

Reflect Using the Principle of Engagement

Because Anthony didn't use information from within the framework to make his instructional decisions, he was not implementing a UDL-focused lesson. But there are some tweaks he can easily make to use the principle of Engagement. Although he introduces the lesson with a video, and students seem to be more likely to pay attention during a video, the question is, did he put anything in place to specifically recruit their interest? Before beginning the video, he could ask the students when they've seen negative and positive numbers outside of the math classroom. It might take the physical prompt of pointing to a thermostat, but some students will recall that the temperature can be shown with negative numbers. Relating to current pop culture, the TV show *The Biggest Loser* has the contestants weigh in at the end of the episode. The number projected is the number of pounds they have gained or lost, so it's a positive or negative number. They might bring up other examples from video games or money examples if they've had those experiences. This quick and simple connection to their lives will help connect them to the video.

Anthony feels compelled to lecture. The checkpoint "foster collaboration and community" might give him the permission he needs to move away from a consistent lecture format. The think-pair-share strategy is a quick way for students to clarify their connection to the information and to get answers from peers. Also, students do not gain the skills necessary to be independently driven learners through the act of lecture. This is not to say that there is never a time for direct instruction such as lecture but that there needs to be options provided so that students can learn to sustain their effort and persistence around any topic.

Finally, Anthony might be tempted to suggest that his worksheets are the perfect opportunity for students to work on their self-regulation. Although this might be the case, his *reason* for choosing the worksheet had minimal connection to the guideline. His need for grades is functionally and not instructionally driven, as I discussed in the introduction to Section I. He does mention that he'll use the data to show the students how far they've come in two days, but to use the worksheet as a baseline grade automatically places some students at a disadvantage. Even if it's a completion grade, students who do not successfully participate in the lesson (e.g., they're so confused they don't even finish the worksheet) are at a significant disadvantage and will likely disengage from the lessons on integers. Instead, Anthony could offer structures to lead his students toward success such as additional guided practice or graduated assessments that have students demonstrate their knowledge only up to the point where they struggle (e.g., when they get three wrong they are done with the assessment). The assessment still provides baseline data. This guideline connects well to the design of the learning environment. By providing structures that help students monitor their own work and effort, investigate their own strategies for remaining on task or seeking assistance, or identifying their own expectations for learning and how to support them, Anthony could tap into the skills identified by the students to motivate them as they complete their work.

4

REPRESENTATION

> Let's say you are just one sided in the way you like to teach. If you just lecture, or you just give things visually, or you just do things your preferred way you're not going to reach everybody. I know that to successfully implement UDL, we have to realize that not only is every kid different, they're different every day!
>
> —Kim Kennedy, third-grade teacher

One might be tempted to define *representation* as giving students examples of the lesson topic in a lot of different ways. Representation within UDL is really about providing students different experiences to receive the information. This definition extends beyond examples that tend to be teacher centered and expands it to experiences that are student centered.

Representation is about building your students' levels of comprehension. Representation is also about demonstrating the influence other languages have on each other and using different mediums to demonstrate this. Finally, representation is about clearly explaining symbols, vocabulary, or sentence structure through experiences. Through this principle, you supply students with background knowledge when necessary or help them bring background knowledge out of their own heads. You help them see the big ideas, process the information, and see how that information connects to other topics or situations. To begin the process of more deeply understanding Representation, let's look at the recognition network.

REPRESENTATION OVERVIEW: KIM KENNEDY Kim Kennedy's take on Representation stresses the use of multiple approaches, considering variable learners, creating a fun environment, and planning purposefully. Moving beyond learning styles, Kim notices that not only do all learners learn differently, but they learn differently within different situations and environments. That's why it's so important to use the UDL framework to design lessons rather than assigning a learner type to each child.

THE RECOGNITION NETWORKS

The recognition networks help us identify patterns related to our senses. These networks not only allow us to identify what is around us and make sense of it but they also allow us to make sense of complex concepts (Rose & Meyer, 2002). For example, our ability to look at a close-up picture of the cartoon character Snoopy's face, recognize the character as a dog, further recall that he is a beagle (even though he doesn't look much like a beagle), and recall what the rest of his body looks like is the remarkable way our recognition networks work. These vast and complex networks present significant implications for the classroom.

How information is presented to students can expand or limit whether or not they learn it. That statement is very straightforward and seems preposterously obvious, but let's take the example of text-based information. Some students do not learn from simple text—the basis for learning as experienced by previous generations. Even today, the majority of information comes to our students in text, and we are expected to move our students beyond the basic comprehension of that text.

The Common Core State Standards (CCSS) emphasize textual analysis (Calkins, Ehrenworth, & Lehman, 2012). These same authors believe that the CCSS redefines reading to be an act in which the reader absorbs and then transforms the information based on individual experiences (Scholes, 1989). Now the comprehension of that textual information becomes more subjective because it is based on each student's background knowledge. This means our students will need support as they journey toward accomplishing these standards.

The principle of Representation introduces us to ways we can provide students access to the ideas, concepts, and themes present within text-based information. At the same time, we can provide support for decoding that information. When students can gain comprehension while working on their decoding, they can move more rapidly toward grasping meaning and then owning the information to use in other contexts or in other situations.

Provide Multiple Means of

Representation

Resourceful, knowledgeable learners

Provide options for comprehension

+ Activate or supply background knowledge
+ Highlight patterns, critical features, big ideas, and relationships
+ Guide information processing, visualization, and manipulation
+ Maximize transfer and generalization

Provide options for language, mathematical expressions, and symbols

+ Clarify vocabulary and symbols
+ Clarify syntax and structure
+ Support decoding of text, mathematical notation, and symbols
+ Promote understanding across languages
+ Illustrate through multiple media

Provide options for perception

+ Offer ways of customizing the display of information
+ Offer alternatives for auditory information
+ Offer alternatives for visual information

Figure 4.1. CAST's principle of Representation.
From Meyer, A., Rose, D.H., & Gordon, D.T. [2013]. *Universal design for learning theory and practice.* Wakefield, MA: National Center on Universal Design for Learning; adapted by permission.

THE PRINCIPLE, GUIDELINES, AND CHECKPOINTS

Of the three principles, the teachers I've worked with seem to be most comfortable with this one. Maybe it's because the basis of Representation is the act of teaching. It's what most of us thought we'd be doing when we dreamed of being teachers. We would be sharing information with students. But how do you share that information? And how do you decide which tools, resources, and strategies to use? The guidelines of Representation help you make those decisions. The principle of Representation is structured around three guidelines (see Figure 4.1).

- Providing options for comprehension (moving from background knowledge to larger concepts, working within those larger concepts to gain deeper understanding)

- Providing options for language, mathematical expression, and symbols (supporting students in their understanding of text, numbers, symbols, and language)

- Providing options for perception (options around display and the customization of visual and auditory information)

Provide Options for Comprehension

Students demonstrate their highest level of learning when they can use what they've learned and apply it within other contexts. This guideline targets the essence of student development and maturity as the learner. In fact, when students are provided opportunities to operate within this guideline, they are becoming self-actualized learners.

Activate or Supply Background Knowledge

In Table 4.1 I reference background knowledge, and, in fact, you see background knowledge referenced under the principle of Engagement. When you connect the topic to something the student already knows, the student is able (and is more likely) to want to connect to the lesson. At the same time, it is equally as empowering when you connect the information you are sharing to the content the students have learned in a different class.

Interdisciplinary lessons can have a strong impact, but you have to establish those connections. By default, most interdisciplinary units focus on a specific book, subject, or activity. For example, you might decide to use the book *The True Story of the Three Little Pigs* by Jon Scieszka (1996) as the basis for your fifth-grade math, social studies, and language arts lessons, but you cannot assume that all of your students know the story of the three little pigs. Without that background knowledge, the story has no meaning and cannot be enjoyed. Furthermore, just because you reference the story to guide their learning activities in math (e.g., learning about estimating by estimating the weight of the pigs), social studies (e.g., civic responsibility, civility, and cooperation by considering the wolf's story), and language areas (e.g., working on figurative language) does not mean the students see how those knowledge areas overlap with the other content areas. You will have to make these connections explicit.

Highlight Patterns, Critical Features, Big Ideas, and Relationships

We want our students to learn how to sift through information and find the most important or relevant information. Within our digital age, where information comes to us constantly and quickly (unless we choose to "unplug" for a bit), the most effective among us are able to filter out the unimportant and ineffective information and find the most important and critical information. The student's ability to learn and manipulate knowledge is directly affected by his or her ability to connect those informational points with other learned information to form new ideas.

You can facilitate this kind of learning by creating and showing structures. As you move through this principle, you will read over and over about the need to translate text into other formats to emphasize meaning and opportunities for understanding. This checkpoint asks you to consider supports that will help your students see connections and critical elements. One way to do that is through graphic representations.

Concept maps are a graphical representation used to represent and organize knowledge. Concepts, usually one- or two-word main ideas, are identified by placing them inside of boxes or circles. The boxes are connected using lines and arrows. The lines or arrows also have a single word or short phrase to define the connection between the main ideas (Novak & Cañas, 2008). The graphic of a concept map shown in Figure 4.2 demonstrates both what a concept map looks like and how information is portrayed within a concept map.

This visual representation is in line with this guideline. Instead of gaining the information only by reading an entire article, students have the opportunity to clarify structural relations and explicitly connect them to earlier learned material. Providing students with a concept map helps them see those larger concepts and identify

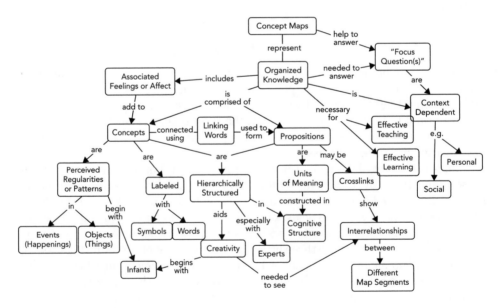

Figure 4.2. A concept map of concept mapping.

From Novak, J.D., & Cañas, A.J. [2008]. *The theory underlying concept maps and how to construct and use them [Technical Report IHMC CmapTools 2006-01 Rev 01-2008].* Pensacola, FL: Florida Institute for Human Machine and Cognition; reprinted by permission. Retrieved from http://cmap.ihmc.us/Publications/ResearchPapers/TheoryUnderlyingConceptMaps.pdf

connections. Supporting students to create their own concept maps allows the students to experience the identification of these concepts and connections. Touching on the principle of Action and Expression, when students can demonstrate this level of understanding, they have reached this high level of learning.

Concept maps, though, are not the be-all and end-all in demonstrating relationships and key ideas. Some students will be bewildered by concept maps. They will find them visually confusing and frustrating. Most of us grew up having to create outlines and are familiar with that construct. Introducing these students to the outline format might help them gain and communicate the same knowledge.

This checkpoint also moves the idea of background knowledge from recognition to use. When students can use knowledge they've gained previously to solve a current problem, they are being resourceful. You can't expect them to do this on their own, though, and this is another area where scaffolding is useful, as demonstrated in the following scenario:

During a first semester unit, students looked at the complex cultural issues during the American Revolution. The United States was creating its own culture, independent of England. Colonists were forced into being resourceful when it came to finding necessary food and creating shelter and goods, and they established their own systems of barter, expectations, and interaction that were different than what was experienced in England. Your students went on to identify cultural underpinnings that articulated conflict between the colonists and English. Now the students are studying the Civil War. You want them to be able to identify the cultural underpinnings that existed in the Northern versus Southern states. While some of your students will be able to remember how they came to identify those during the American Revolution unit, others will need prompts.

If you are implementing UDL during the American Revolution unit, you will have diagrams, pictures, maps, and other visual products created by you and the students to which you can refer to remind them of those discussions. These products become examples that act as a prompt or can be used to create scaffolding. Nonexamples can also be helpful to clarify ideas, especially when you are teaching about nonliteral issues, such as cultural underpinnings. Your use of these products can help awaken the students' background knowledge and act as scaffolds throughout the lesson.

Guide Information Processing, Visualization, and Manipulation

Successful learners are able to take information and organize it. That might mean summarizing, prioritizing, categorizing, or identifying a context. Some students, though, might need guidance in gaining this skill. That guidance needs to be direct, structured, and scaffolded.

Some students do not immediately identify sequential steps and thus need scaffolding. A popular writing prompt that addresses this is the creation of a peanut butter and jelly sandwich. You ask the students to write down, step-by-step, how to make a peanut butter and jelly sandwich (the bread, jar of peanut butter, jar of jelly, and knife are already on the counter). The more specific they can be the better. Before beginning this next step, you should ensure you have no students with peanut allergies in your class; you can create another type of sandwich if this is the case. You then use their directions to make a sandwich. I recommend not announcing whose directions you're using to minimize embarrassment if the directions are not thorough enough. Once they have seen you try to make the sandwich, more students will become more specific with their steps. Others might need some scaffolding, and there are a variety of ways you can provide that.

You can create a word bank of steps to creating the sandwich, from which they can choose; you can organize that word bank into three groups that the students would put in order (chunking the information); you can establish that there are 15 steps; you can provide the information for every fifth step and have the students fill in the other steps (a progressive release of the information); or you can provide prompts such as, "Is the top already off of the peanut butter jar?" This gives the students multiple ways to enter the activity. The point is to help the students become stronger organizers of information. Providing prompts can help them move further down that learning path. Although this is a popular prompt, you might have students in your classroom who have never had a peanut butter and jelly sandwich because of family preference, culture, or allergies (as noted previously). Even this kind of activity needs a quick check on background knowledge.

Another reason this is a nice example is that this checkpoint suggests you provide interactive models. These models are opportunities for students to observe or participate in the organization of information. While this example can be overlaid on any sequential activity, the scaffolding can be transferred to activities in which students are asked to summarize, prioritize or categorize information. For your students who are highly proficient with this skill and who finish quickly, you can deepen their learning and self-exploration. They need to investigate the processes they use to organize the information. When students can communicate how they work through a process they not only have ownership of it, they are more likely able to apply it to other situations and can potentially support others as they learn the process.

MAXIMIZE TRANSFER AND GENERALIZATION

Being able to take information from one situation and transfer it to another demonstrates a deeper understanding of the information. For example, young students might first hear about the role chlorophyll has in creating the green leaves on trees. This can be as early as first or second grade. When they hear about chlorophyll again they are likely talking about all green plants. The desire is that students can transfer what they learned about chlorophyll in relation to the green leaves on the trees to the green leaves on other plants. If so, they have both transferred the information to a new context and setting and generalized the information from the trees to other green plants. What makes transfer and generalization most successful from a teacher's point of view is to remember that no knowledge can be retained in isolation. When it is connected to larger concepts and is demonstrated to be interconnected to other situations, contexts, and relationships it is more likely to take on relevancy to the student. This is why project-based learning (PBL) can be so successful when designed with UDL in mind.

PBL is a learning construct guided by projects, designed around complex tasks, resulting in realistic products, events, or presentations. These products directly tie back to the curriculum. Each project is governed by a driving question which relates to a discipline's concepts or curriculum components. Students involved in PBL design and manage their work as they become involved in knowledge building, inquiry, investigation, and resolution. They gain factual knowledge that researchers find to be equivalent or superior to that gained by students involved in traditional learning (Thomas, 2000; Vega, 2012). Other researchers found that long-term retention, skill development, and the satisfaction of students and teachers were higher in PBL environments than in traditional instructional environments (Strobel & van Barneveld, 2009).

Outside of PBL, there are strategies that you can use to help your students gain a stronger connection to the material. Grounding it in previous knowledge or familiar and current experiences is a beginning, but the deeper connection comes when students can say how the new knowledge affects their former or current experiences and knowledge. They might not see the automatic connection, though.

If your students are learning about typography in art class (understanding how the size and shape of letters can affect both the information being shared and the person reading the information), you can have them create the letters of their name to represent hobbies, likes, and experiences. For example, within the name Violet, an "o" might be the wheel of a bicycle and an "I" might be a clarinet. This would provide the students with explicit practice to understand the concept and purpose of typography.

The goal is for the transfer and generalization to occur when the students learn about the importance of media throughout time, from the formalized writing of the Greeks and Romans to the design of today's web sites, and that typography has remained with us. If the art and social studies teachers have been in contact, the social studies teacher can refer back to the art project. Then, using the checkpoint of "clarifying vocabulary and symbols" the social studies teacher could break down the word *typography* to the study of type and have students identify where they see different fonts within the classroom.

Transfer and generalization can occur within a single year or across several years. It will take looking for those opportunities to tie information back to something they learned previously. Other supports include using mnemonic devices, other memory strategies, and opportunities for specific practice.

RESOURCEFUL LEARNERS: KIM KENNEDY AND LEARNING STRATEGIES Kim Kennedy believes the most resourceful and knowledgeable learners are those who help one another transfer and generalize information. To help her third-grade students reach this level, she demonstrates a strategy and then has students practice so they can eventually utilize those strategies on their own and during collaborative activities. Other supports include: using mnemonic devices, other memory strategies, and opportunities for specific practice.

Provide Options for Language, Mathematical Expressions, and Symbols

Written language includes more than letters. How those letters are combined to create language can require clarification. This guideline breaks down the components of transmitted language across the content areas (e.g., English, math, science) and across languages (e.g., English, Spanish, Japanese).

TRANSFERRING INFORMATION: KIM KENNEDY AND TEACHING CHALLENGING CONCEPTS   Students have a difficult time taking concepts from examples and applying them. To help teach the concepts of acute and obtuse angles to her third-graders, Kim Kennedy uses a singsong voice, physical actions, and rhyming sayings to not only capture the attention of her students, but to help them learn memorable phrases they can use to trigger their memory. She gives them the example and has them participate using the same motions and voice. For example, she uses the phrase, "Acute and tiny less than 90" in a high pitched voice while holding her thumb and finger at an angle less than 90 degrees. The students copy her movements and voice. Then she stands up straight with her hands on either side of her chest. While saying the word "obtuse" with a very low voice, she pushes out her chest and opens her arms wide. The students gleefully copy her movements and voice again. She encourages them to use these motions and voices as needed so they can remember the information. Gradually, the students become familiar enough with the concepts that they discontinue using the sayings and movements. She's had students who recall "acute and tiny, less than 90" during other math lessons on greater than and less than symbols, demonstrating their transfer of that knowledge.

Clarify Vocabulary and Symbols

This checkpoint digs into the supports you want to provide so your students can connect to the vocabulary and symbols, see how complex groupings of vocabulary or symbols break down, and understand challenging references in the text. Hinging on background knowledge, this checkpoint addresses the preteaching you do to prep your students for new vocabulary and symbols. This preteaching doesn't necessarily happen just at the beginning of the lesson, though. Preteaching occurs whenever you are introducing a new concept, word, or symbol and you want to ensure that all of your students are prepared to move forward.

In a lesson about the greater-than and less-than symbols, I have seen teachers call the symbol a mouth and use objects such as cookies to represent the numbers. After putting three cookies in one pile and five cookies in the other, the teacher asks the students which way the mouth faces if the mouth likes cookies and wants more cookies.

The lesson continues to create depth, but the teacher uses two representations familiar with students to introduce them to the mathematical symbol and concept.

Complex vocabulary is present within all languages. While it's automatic to consider complex words (i.e., vocabulary beyond the scope of the student's understanding or their current personal bank of words), this checkpoint also suggests that we consider groupings of words such as idioms, figurative language, colloquialisms, or jargon. These same groups can occur in math and science too, taking the format of equations, properties, and theorems. Providing your students with opportunities to familiarize themselves with these groupings is valuable. You can break down this language for your students into simpler words and symbols, building on their vocabulary. Allowing students the time to explore these concepts, words, and groupings together is invaluable. Often, the conversations they have among themselves can bring more understanding than your descriptions.

When addressing the CCSS K-5 Language Standards for Grade 2 under Vocabulary Acquisition and Use, it would be helpful to consider this checkpoint. The standard reads, "Determine or clarify the meaning of unknown and multiple-meaning words and phrases based on grade 2 reading and content, choosing flexibility from an array of strategies." The standard is further specified with: "(c) Use a root word as a clue to the meaning of an unknown word with the same root (e.g., addition, additional)" (National Governors Association Center for Best Practices & Council of Chief State School Officers, 2010, p. 27).

Table 4.1 lists several different ways you can guide students to first identify the root word and then move on to identifying the meaning of the word. The purpose of the activity is also given.

Table 4.1. Word meaning

Activity: Make sure students have the opportunity to see and hear the root alongside the complex word.

Purpose: Background knowledge

Activity: Write word on the board in one color. Next, write the word with the root word emphasized with another color, a different font, or a different size.

Purpose: Background knowledge

Activity: Affix the root word to the board or wall using a magnet or tape. Emphasize it as the root. Affix the prefix or suffix to the board or wall to show the students the more complex word. Ask the students to tell you which one is the root word.

Purpose: Background knowledge

Activity: Pass out note cards with the prefix or suffix and the root word paper clipped together. Have students lay out the word on their desks. For your quick check, they will act out, draw, or verbally describe the meaning of the complex word. Students clip the two note cards back together and trade with another student to repeat the activity. You can repeat this activity several times to offer practice with minimal prep (you only have to make the number of complex word pairs as there are students).

Purpose: Movement toward standard

Activity: Post sentences using complex words (e.g., The lion was circling his prey) along with a picture or video demonstrating the meaning of the sentence. Ensure students understand the word "prey," then ask them to identify the meaning of "circling," the root word of "circle," and connect the two. Repeat with other examples.

Purpose: Movement toward standard

Finally, technology is helpful with this checkpoint. Students' ability to hyperlink to definitions, look up the different groupings, and then share that information through class web sites or school-based social networking sites assists them in their understanding. Helping the students use the technology wisely is imperative. Guiding them in finding appropriate web sites with quality information can help them grow in their independence as learners (Eagleton, Guinee, & Langlais, 2009).

Clarify Syntax and Structure

 Syntax relates to the rules of language (i.e., grammar or sentence structure) and these are present in both language and math. They can also be present in the other ways language is represented, as addressed previously (e.g., graphic representation, narratives). This checkpoint focuses on clarifying structural relations and explicitly connecting them to earlier learned material. To me, there is a micro and macro part of this checkpoint. The micro is occurring when students are learning the actual grammatical or mathematical rules. For example, before students can learn the difference between a prepositional phrase and a participle phrase, they must learn what a preposition is versus a participle. That's the micro part. Now that they have that information, they can learn about the structure of the phrases (both begin with either a preposition or a participle). To go macro, though, you will emphasize to them the previously learned information. You'll be blending this checkpoint with others as you physically highlight, underline, or write in unique letters those prepositions or participles. You will very purposefully point out to them the piece that they've learned about previously.

This checkpoint also points to the structural relationship within the language or math formula and making relationships within that relationship clear. This is another instance where a concept map or other visual organizer could be helpful. Identifying the connection between the concepts is of key importance within this checkpoint.

Support Decoding of Text, Mathematical Notation, and Symbols

 The ability to decode information, whether it is in a textual, numeric, symbolic, or Braille format takes extensive practice. For some, additional supports are needed that range from the identification of key concepts to vocal supports. Today's technology provides many of these vocal supports. The text-to-speech supports available on laptops and desktops have improved greatly. This is, however, not exhaustive of the other handheld technologies available, including tablets and smart phones. Some available programming can offer voicing with digital mathematical notation (called Math ML). Other programming is written to use a recording of a human voice to support the text.

If you have access to tapes and tape recorders, a lower tech option is to record yourself or someone else reading the information for the students. The no-tech option is reading the information out loud at the moment. This is where reading buddies can become a powerful tool within your classroom, and don't forget math, as in the following scenario.

Mike's fifth-grade classroom was in the midst of a math lesson. The students were in small groups and had workbooks open in front of them but were paying attention to his demonstration on the overhead. He was using overlay tiles to demonstrate fractions and decimals, the same activity the students were going to do at their desks. He emphasized the key concepts, words, and symbols they would be talking about in their small groups. Together, they vocalized the terms through choral responses (e.g., he said "numerator" then "denominator" while pointing to the corresponding number. The students then did the same when he pointed to the corresponding number). When the time came for them to work in their small groups, he asked specific students in each group to read the problems aloud, including the mathematical notation. Although none of the students in that classroom had low or no vision, Mike wanted all of his students to have the benefit of hearing the mathematical notation and experiencing the similarities between .20, 1/5, and a circle graph with one of the five pieces shaded in. Once the leaders had read a few problems, the task rotated to other students in the group. Students supported one another in their verbal enunciation of the fractions and decimals. He circulated to support their verbalized decoding.

Promote Understanding Across Languages

Many of us have had experiences with learners for whom English is not their primary language (e.g., English language learners [ELLs], students who are deaf). While most experience the former, both groups need similar supports, including access to translation tools and situation–content–domain specific vocabulary. For example, kindergarten students learn the names of colors. Providing the students with the names of the colors in their native language along with the word in English helps bridge the knowledge gap. Later, if they are reading a story and colors are written within the story (e.g., The yellow bus is at school), you can highlight the word *yellow* with a yellow highlighter to trigger their memory of the color and associate it with the word. Furner, Yahya, and Duffy (2005) provide suggestions that align with this checkpoint and can benefit students who are English language learners and students with disabilities related to learning:

- Teach vocabulary through concrete objects and demonstration.

- Relate math problems and vocabulary to background knowledge.

- Apply problems to daily life situations.

- Use manipulatives to make problems concrete.

- Encourage drawings to translate and visualize word problems.

- Have English language learner/students with disabilities related to learning pair with typical students for computer/cooperative activities.

- Explain directions clearly and repeat key terms.

- Group students heterogeneously during cooperative learning.

- Make interdisciplinary connections to what students are learning in math.

- Make cultural connections for students when teaching mathematics.

- Rewrite word problems in simple terms.

- Create word bank charts and hang them in the classroom for viewing.

Using auditory, visual, and kinesthetic teaching approaches for different learning styles enables teachers to reach more students than the traditional direct-instruction or paper-and-pencil drill and practice forms of instruction (Furner et al., 2005).

Although there are several strategies that support both of these generalized populations, there are some areas that require more specific attention to English language learners. In relation to math, there are several differences between the United States and international settings. Money and the metric system are significant areas. People in the United States identify decimals by using a period. In South America and many other European countries, they use a comma, and vice versa (Furner et al., 2005). For example, our notation for four and thirty-six hundredths is: 4.36. In these other locations, it would be written 4,36. Additional tips are summarized in Table 4.2.

Table 4.2. English language learning strategies

Strategy: The use of interactive styles such as going directly to the student's desk to offer quiet support (teacher interacting with students) (Curtin, 2005).

Related outcome: Students felt more appreciated and involved.

Universal design for learning checkpoint: Engagement. Providing options for sustaining effort and persistence.

Strategy: The use of multiple examples to illustrate content (Curtin, 2005).

Related outcome: Students felt more appreciated and involved.

Universal design for learning checkpoint: Representation. Provide options for perception and provide options for language, mathematical expressions, and symbols.

Strategy: The teacher speaks slowly and gives directions in small quantities (Curtin, 2005).

Related outcome: Students felt more appreciated and involved.

Universal design for learning checkpoint: Representation: Provide options for perception and provide options for language, mathematical expressions, and symbols and provide options for comprehension.

Strategy: Multicultural influences are woven through the curriculum (Craighead & Ramanathan, 2007; Gay, 2000; Nieto, 2004)

Related outcome: Students make connections between personal experiences and new content.

Universal design for learning checkpoint: Representation. Provide options for language, mathematical expression, and symbols.

Strategy: Validating students' culture and language through the rich use of multicultural resources and language.

Related outcome: " . . . for students still learning English, taking advantage of the native language can speed the acquisition of English and make it possible to continue to learn school subjects while still improving English" (Tse, 2001, p. 44).

Universal design for learning checkpoint: Representation. Provide options for language, mathematical expression, and symbols.

Strategy: Learning basic greetings and popular phrases from the student's primary language, but you don't have to be fluent.

Related outcome: To the student, this legitimizes his or her language (Ovando & Collier, 1998).

Universal design for learning checkpoint: Representation. Provide options for language, mathematical expression, and symbols

Strategy: Having a library of texts in student's primary language

Related outcome: Affirms the value of primary language (Ovando & Collier, 1998).

Universal design for learning checkpoint: Representation. Provide options for perception and provide options for language, mathematical expression, and symbols.

Source: Craighead and Ramanthan (2007)

These suggestions come from researched strategies known to be effective for English language learners in the general education setting. The deaf community also has a defined culture that has identified best practices (Easterbrooks & Stephenson, 2006) and, in-line with other cultures, students who are deaf have personal cultures (e.g., Black and deaf, Hispanic and deaf, Native American and deaf, Asian Pacific and deaf) that drive the affective piece of their learning (Fletcher-Carter & Paez, 2010). Specific to the table format, because a few of the strategies go beyond this checkpoint, the third column lists the UDL checkpoint addressed by the suggested strategy.

Illustrate Through Multiple Media

This checkpoint suggests supporting what I would label as static text (what you find in a textbook) with another version of that text. That could range from something drawn to something that has movement (including you). What is most important is that the connection is made explicit. Being explicit is extremely important as you begin to consider what examples you want to use.

Identifying the main point/focus of the text/textually based information will help you decide how to symbolically represent the information. Once you have done that, you can choose the medium you would like to use. Photos, diagrams, charts, graphs, graphic representations, tables, and one-dimensional or three-dimensional models are all considerations. Moving into technology, this is where you can use on-line resources to bring the text to life, whether through pictures, videos, diagrams, or graphics. The idea is to recognize that most information in the classroom is still delivered via text. If your students are working on understanding, then that is a key time to provide them with these other options.

Provide Options for Perception

When we think about perception we often limit it to sight, but perception is far broader.

- It can include images we see in our mind, how we feel based on our physical surroundings, how we feel based on an experience, when we experience intuition, and our ability to think through things.

In line with this expansive definition, the checkpoints of this guideline help to further define and structure the depth of this definition. In the following examples, I highlight both low-tech and technology-based ideas.

> **GUIDING INFORMATION PROCESSING: KIM KENNEDY AND VISUAL PROMPTS** Through the use of morning meetings, posted lesson goals, and visual prompts, Kim Kennedy guides her students' actions and participation during class. By providing these supports, Kim is able to support her third-grade students in their growth toward becoming more resourceful and knowledgeable learners within her collaborative and cooperative classroom. These actions, along with verbal and visual cues, establish an expectation that her students use information around them to operate successfully within that environment.

Offers Ways to Customize the Display of Information

When you customize the display of information, you are thinking about size, shape, color, and brightness. Whatever you're displaying, consider whether it can be shown only as a one-dimensional item or if it can be three dimensional. Under this checkpoint, you're also considering the speed at which the information is provided and how you are positioning and highlighting the information.

A low-tech example of this checkpoint is to use different-colored markers, chalk, pens, or pencils to emphasize different words, numbers, or symbols. If you were to write a sentence on the board and wanted to highlight the prepositional phrase, you might write, "The horse ran down the lane" with "The horse ran" in one color and "down the lane" in another contrasting color. Writing the sentence in that way provides an additional cue or level of support for some of the students in your environment. You can also make the letters more bold, change the size of the words, or even the shape of the letters in this same example and achieve similar results (e.g., using a shadowing technique, bubble letters, placing emphasizing lines around the letters). Planning for students who experience colorblindness or who don't perceive a connection between the colors and sentence structures, the size of the font or emphasizing the font might be a better choice. In this case, you would want to make the difference fairly significant versus subtle.

Moving beyond text or numbers, consider any graphics you're showing. Graphics might include maps, tables, diagrams, graphs, or even a musical score as in the following example:

Tami's students were learning how to tap out rhythms based on a musical score with quarter notes, half notes, and whole notes. Some of her students were experiencing significant struggles in seeing the difference between the quarter notes and the half notes within the score. Pausing, Tami reflected on the goal of her lesson (discussed in Chapter 6); "Students will demonstrate a rhythm that uses quarter, half and whole notes." To ensure their confusion wasn't based on misreading the notes, Tami took 8 1/2-inch x 11-inch pieces of paper and drew a quarter note on a staff that filled one sheet. On another, she drew a half note on a staff in the same size.

On the third piece of paper, she drew the whole note on a staff. She began by holding up the half note and asking the students to point to the half note in their score. They then practiced clapping and counting the length of that note. She followed this same process with the other two rhythmic representations. Although there were more things that she did to support her students' knowledge of quarter, half, and whole notes, by creating larger representations of the notes, she used this checkpoint.

Within the realm of technology, different hardware and software can help you address this checkpoint. In many cases, educational companies embed these capabilities into their hardware and software. Instead of having students read from a textbook or a printed article, accessing this information through a reader can bring the text to life, as long as that flexibility is built into the product (e.g., different colors, bolded words, the ability to enlarge the text). Simply posting a PDF online for students to access does not address this checkpoint because the way the information is displayed is identical to the way they would see it on a sheet of paper. To check the technology you're choosing against this checkpoint, consider whether the text, graphics, or color can be altered; whether the information can be backlit; or if information can be highlighted.

Offer Alternatives for Auditory Information

 Auditory information is information you can hear. When an individual has limited hearing or is deaf, there are supports we automatically consider: captioning, transcripts, American Sign Language, tactile supports (e.g., student holds percussion instrument while person with hearing plays the rhythm), visual representations of the

Table 4.3. From verbal to visual

Verbal request: Scenario. Students are moving around the classroom and lining up for recess. Request: "Be sure to go to the gym after recess today."

How to offer it visually: You have the schedule for the day written on the board. You physically walk to the board and point to the change in the schedule. For students who need even more support, you use pictures to represent the schedule and place the picture representing gym in the spot after recess.

Verbal request: Scenario. It's the end of the day and students are packing up. Request: "Picture money is due tomorrow."

How to offer it visually: You have a section of your board reserved for announcements. There aren't always announcements, so you make sure to stand next to the announcement area and point to this new item. For students who need more support, you place a brightly colored piece of paper with this information within their notebook or backpack.

Verbal request: Scenario. Class is starting, students are seated, and they are pulling their books and folders out of their backpacks. Request: "Turn to page 17 in your textbook."

How to offer it visually: You have written the page number at the top of the overhead or board in a consistent location so students know where to find the information.

Verbal request: Scenario. Students are involved in a think-pair-share exercise (they think about the topic on their own, move into pairs, and share their thoughts or answers with the other person. The purpose is to gain anothers' perspective and build knowledge). Request: "Make sure you write your partner's complete answer down so you can both get credit."

How to offer it visually: Whether this is a request consistent with how you always manage this activity or if it is an add on, you give each pair of students this information on an instruction sheet that is specific to the activity. If paper is at a minimum, you write this guideline on the board and ensure students look at the information as you read it aloud.

sound (e.g., images that represent the music), or visual representations of the information (e.g., charts, graphs). There are also students whose hearing is not affected but who would benefit from those and other supports. These students struggle when information is presented to them verbally (see Table 4.3). However, although it is rare that any of us only lecture, there are many actions embedded within the life of a classroom that might only be provided verbally.

If you are an experienced teacher, you likely saw a theme in the previous suggestions. First, consistency was mentioned in the first three. Designing a learning environment with systematic and consistent characteristics will support your learners. While you can change the arrangement of your desks, require students to work with different peers, position yourself in different areas throughout the room, you should consider what information the students need to know each day to be effective learners. This gets a bit into other guideline areas, but by visually posting necessary information, you are improving your students' opportunities to access the information. Second, you positioned your body next to the information. This is a best practice that benefits individuals in the deaf and hard-of-hearing community, but it also emphasizes the information to all of your students.

Offer Alternatives for Visual Information

An initial question might be how this checkpoint differs from "customizing the display of information." When you customize the information, you are using the text or graphic that is offered and altering it. Under this checkpoint, you are considering other ways to communicate and possibly to enhance the visual information. These methods might be auditory cues, physical objects, or descriptions.

When I was a young child, my parents purchased for me little paperback books that came with a small record. When I played the record I heard the story read to me, but my favorite part was the ding of a bell that told me to turn the page. This is an example of an auditory cue. As a beginning reader, I might or might not have been decoding the written words with my own eyes, but I did pick up on the fact that it was time to turn the page when I heard that bell ring.

You can use auditory cues to demonstrate times for transition that might otherwise be embedded within written instructions (e.g., beginning or ending activities, changing spaces within the classroom, entering or leaving a space, beginning or stopping a conversation). Some of these suggestions lean toward classroom management ideas, but they are also instances when some students need additional cues to help them realize it's time for a transition.

Physical objects can become supports when they demonstrate how ideas intersect or what they might mean. Take, for example, the following checkpoint represented within a zoology lesson:

Brian's students are reading about amphibians as an introduction to a unit on frogs. They will be dissecting the frogs in about a week, and he wants to be sure they understand the general characteristics of this species' class. While his students can read about these characteristics, he feels it is more valuable for them to examine them visually. Fortunately, he has access to examples from the four groups (orders) of amphibians. The students have the opportunity to move from example to example and write down and/or discuss what they see in common between the four examples. These physical objects assist some students in identifying the similarities.

Physical objects can also help students gain a better understanding of spatial relations. Although you can provide an excellent written description of a space or how an item fits within a space, providing an image or model that can be manipulated can assist in understanding. Something as straightforward as passing around golf balls, tennis balls, baseballs, and basketballs to communicate the concept of a sphere addresses this checkpoint.

Finally, while we all have heard the adage that a picture speaks a thousand words, there are many reasons why a student might not come up with those words. If you are using an image, graphic, or video to convey a message, supporting them with descriptions will help ensure you are reaching your students. Consider a cartoon with three panels. There is action to communicate a message, but what is communicated to you is likely different than what will be communicated to your students because of the difference in experiences. By using written or spoken words, you clarify the message. Let's say your students are looking at a picture from the weekly student newspaper to which you subscribe. The picture is there to support the text, but you might need to provide additional text or spoken descriptions to ensure your students see the connection to the article.

CONCLUSION

The principle of Representation is designed to guide teachers in the design of the information being shared. When all students are given the opportunity to grasp the concepts or information in a variety of ways, they are more likely to gain and maintain that knowledge. Most important, they will be able to eventually use that knowledge in other areas of learning and life. This is the ultimate quest for us as teachers under this principle.

Revisiting Anthony's Lesson

Anthony's lesson was about adding integers. Because this was the first day of the topic, he found a short cartoon video in which the characters were numbers and talked through what it meant to be an integer. It showed them sitting on a number line and how they combined through addition. He gave each student a number line to use and keep in his or her folder and then followed up with a worksheet. Students worked independently, and he went to their desks if they had questions.

This sounds like a UDL lesson, doesn't it? Anthony had a cartoon video, so the students must have been engaged. Add that to the number lines at their desks, and he must have been representing the information to them. Then they worked on a worksheet. That's expression, right? This must be a UDL lesson!

Let's interview Anthony about this lesson.

Loui: "Hi Anthony. Thanks for answering some questions about your lesson."

(continued)

(continued)

Anthony:	"Sure thing!"
Loui:	"I'm curious why you chose that video."
Anthony:	"We all know kids love the cartoon videos and I thought the cartoon did a great job of introducing integers."
Loui:	"It did look like they enjoyed it. Now, you followed that up with some additional instruction, and then the students worked on their worksheets. Can you tell me why you chose those activities?"
Anthony:	"Well, I always follow a video with a lecture. Otherwise, I'm not teaching, right? The students have to hear and see me teach or else I'm not doing my job. Then, I wanted to see if they were getting it, so I gave them the worksheets. I needed some more scores for the grade book, and those need to be individual scores. This way, I can show where they started and then how much growth they have achieved in the next two days as we work on integers. I can't get those scores from group work because that's not fair to all of the students."

Reflect Using the Principle of Representation

While Anthony's lesson did use a video to introduce the lesson, there's no way to know the quality of the video. What we hope is that the video clearly laid out what an integer is and where an integer is placed on a number line, depending on the negative symbol or no negative symbol. If so, it's possible that Anthony did provide alternatives for auditory and visual information (provide options for perception). What we also couldn't see in this lesson was whether or not he connected integers to previous conversations about negative numbers. How did the students come to that knowledge, and did he remind them of negative numbers using those triggers (e.g., they would hold their arm up in front of them, elbow bent so that their arm came across their body to signify a negative sign)? They could use this to create a physical number line.

Another possibility would be a number line without digits stretched across the floor (yarn and masking tape can achieve this). Students are given papers with whole numbers written on them and told whether they are positive or negative. The students with negative numbers hold their arms up as negative signs and position themselves on the line. This physical interaction can help some students connect with the concept of a number line (provide options for language, mathematical expressions, and symbols).

By reviewing Anthony's lesson against the principle of Representation, we can see that there are many more avenues that can be traveled. As long as he knows what tools and resources he already has available to him, he can match those along with known strategies to the three guidelines to build more learning opportunities for a wider range of students.

5

ACTION AND EXPRESSION

I know I've taught a successful universal design for learning (UDL)–based lesson when my students can show me what they've learned through some sort of assessment. Whether it's through pencil and paper or technology, there is an end product. Whether that's performance based, orally, theatrically, or a PowerPoint, it's however they can explain it, even a test. I open that door to let them show me what they learned. Also, that student who struggles, if he or she gets it, then I know I was successful because I hit their learning need as well. When all of this happens I know it was presented in multiple ways and they got it.

—Kim Kennedy, third-grade teacher

We feel good when our students demonstrate their knowledge. It doesn't matter if you are in the K–12 environment, the postsecondary environment, or a teaching environment outside of the traditional classroom, when your students experience that "ah-ha" moment and then excitedly express their new knowledge, you experience satisfaction. It's part of what makes teaching so fulfilling. Sometimes, though, we find ourselves limiting the number of opportunities or ways students can demonstrate their knowledge. The more we open up those options and opportunities, the more "ah-ha" moments we get to witness. When we allow our students to show what they know, they move toward becoming strategic and goal-directed learners (Meyer, Rose, & Gordon, 2013).

IMPORTANCE OF ACTION AND EXPRESSION: LAURIE MARTIN   Laurie Martin sees why the principle of Action and Expression is so important in the classroom. She views the principle of Representation as the work performed by the teacher and the principle of Action and Expression as the work generated by her middle school students. That interpretation of the principle allows her to see her students' level of understanding and whether or not they have connected with the goal of the lesson.

The principle of Action and Expression is about providing opportunities to students as they practice goal setting, planning, strategy building, organizing and using information and resources, and monitoring their own progress in these areas.

Action and Expression encourages teachers to include physical interaction, the use of both high-tech and low- or no-tech tools, and structures that lead to student self-management so students can fully demonstrate their knowledge. Action and Expression is also about providing students with opportunities to demonstrate what they know through a variety of acts or creations. These can include physical actions, media, the construction of objects, and writing.

In Chapter 2 I wrote that the teacher designs the learning environment. In the case of Action and Expression, that environmental design can include the use or formative and/or summative assessments. Formative evaluations are designed to take a snapshot of the students' progress along the way and help the teacher gauge whether or not the student is learning the information and actively shift their instruction. For some, though, assessments are limited to the end of the lesson or unit. They are a way to identify whether or not students learned the information. In an environment designed using UDL, assessments are used to inform the teacher on where students stand in their understanding and to use that information to make changes to the learning environment so students can successfully acquire the information.

TYPES OF ASSESSMENTS

Assessment is feedback. Depending on the type of assessment given and how the subsequent information is used, the process of assessment can create a *feedback loop*. Most commonly viewed as a part of communication, a feedback loop confirms what information has been shared and that everyone involved has interpreted the information similarly. Translated to the classroom, the way you design and implement lessons determines what opportunities your students will have to learn. If the learning environment you create incorporates the feedback loop, then your assessments provide critical information that you can use to adjust lessons, and your students gain skills in adjusting their efforts. These two steps allow both teacher and students to move toward desired outcomes. The feedback loop is what makes formative assessments come to life.

Formative Assessments

An assessment becomes a formative assessment when the evidence is used by both the students and the teacher. Students use them to assess their learning and teachers use them to adapt how they are meeting the needs of the students (Andrade, Huff, & Brooke, 2012; Brookhart, 2007; Clark, 2010; Harlen & James, 1997). Inherent to formative assessment is the feedback loop; students and teachers adapt based on the outcomes of that assessment. These types of assessments demonstrate the small steps forward or the small missteps students are taking in their development. By assessing these small steps teachers can redirect the students by using scaffolding, reteaching strategies, and feedback. The student role is equally as important as students learn to use that same information to gauge their learning.

Formative evaluations can use any type of design (e.g., verbal, hands on, multiple choice, essay, games). If students demonstrate disconnect from what was taught, teachers adjust current lessons, subsequent lessons, or provide other follow-up support. However, without these actions, the act of formative assessment is not complete (Black & William, 1998).

When designed effectively, administered well, and followed up using mastery-oriented feedback, formative assessments can be a more accurate measure of current student knowledge (Harlen & James, 1997; Brookhart, 2012). Certain elements need to be considered, however. A well-designed formative assessment takes into account the wide variety of needs, preferences, and strengths within the learning environment, and it takes into account the variable learners. It is based on what the students are currently learning but also can include an assessment of student effort and progress made over time. Because students' individual needs and learning behaviors are taken into account, encouragement and specific guidance can be offered. This means it will not be a single multiple-choice assessment, but there will be different types of brief assessments over the course of the lesson where students show what they know.

Summative Assessments

Summative assessments as a whole demonstrate the students' ability to retain significant amounts of information and manipulate it to fit with the assessment's questions or prompts. This is a traditional approach to gauging whether a student has fully understood the course or topic content and can demonstrate that understanding. Summative evaluations can also use any type of design (e.g., verbal, hands on, multiple choice, essay, games); however, they tend to focus on pen-and-paper and, in some cases, online designs.

Large-scale summative assessments are typically designed to be standardized and cumulative with the purpose of categorizing the achievement of the student, and they tend to occur at the end of a lesson, unit, grading term, semester, or after a longer period of time. That information is used by educators and policy makers to make curricular and instructional decisions (Andrade et al., 2012). When viewed as a part of a system, formative and summative assessments together can offer direction to educators and policymakers (Andrade et al., 2012). This is where UDL fits within the discussion.

Most people relate the word *standard* to the statewide or national exams given to students throughout their time in the K–12 environment. However, any time a classroom assessment is designed so that all students are required to answer the same questions in the same way, students are participating in a standardized format. In the next section you will read how UDL encourages teachers to provide

UNIVERSAL DESIGN FOR LEARNING AND STANDARDIZED TESTS: LAURIE MARTIN AND STUDENT PREPARATION According to Laurie Martin, there is a relationship between her middle school students successfully completing statewide standardized tests and UDL. By creating standards-based lessons which use the UDL framework, teachers provide multiple pathways to students as they acquire the skills related to the standards. In Laurie's experience, this use of the UDL framework helps students prepare for the upcoming assessments without putting them through drills and memorization.

students with opportunities to show what they know through a variety of assessment designs and the varietal use of tools, resources, and strategies. However, I have heard the questions "How do I get them ready for the test?" and "Don't they have to practice taking standardized tests to show that they can do it?" In other words, how does it all mesh?

Universal Design for Learning and Assessments

Students benefit from understanding the structure and layout of standardized tests and the strategies used during test taking (e.g., first, eliminate the answers you know to be completely wrong and then use contextual clues to make decisions about the leftover answers), but competency is at the heart of the previous questions. Students need to know the information *and* be able to use it as required by the exam.

This connects to the guidelines "provide options for self-regulation," under Engagement, and "provide options for comprehension," under Representation. The first guideline emphasizes the students' ability to use personal coping skills and to reflect on their learning. The second guideline suggests that students have opportunities to use their background knowledge; identify and use the patterns, critical features, big ideas, and relationships they recognize; process, visualize, and manipulate information; and take pieces of information they have learned and apply it to other settings or topics. These are exactly the skills they need to activate during a summative assessment. In addition, students activate their executive functions, which you will read about later in this chapter. Whether that is a classroom-based or a state or national assessment, these are all skills your students will need to use to be successful on a summative assessment.

It can be challenging to shift from a purely summative environment to one that more frequently uses formative assessment. The following scenario about LaSandra's class shows how using an assessment originally designed to be summative is altered to act as a formative assessment.

LaSandra's sixth-grade students are to take a test about the Mayan culture. All of her students are taking the same assessment, which has multiple-choice and fill-in-the-blank questions and a timeline to complete. She could use this test as a standardized summative assessment, but she chooses to use it formatively. Once they have completed the test, she asks the students to work in pairs or small groups to assess their answers. Her students are used to working in pairs and small groups, and together she and her students have established behavioral expectations in her classroom. In addition, her students have been working on the concept of supporting evidence throughout the year. These pieces are blended into the activity.

LaSandra asks the students pull out a sheet of lined notebook paper and fold it in half lengthwise, which turns the paper into a table with a center line. She has created a guide sheet for the groups to use with the following instructions:

Reminder: This is a collaborative activity. In this classroom, we practice respect, acceptance, and promote each other's learning. How we treat each other is just as important as the information we are learning.

Directions: The group leader will read each question aloud. Each student will have the opportunity to share the answer he or she wrote down. Students will use classroom-based resources to identify the correct answers. Any questions answered incorrectly on the test should be written on the left side of the notebook paper. The correct answer and supporting evidence should be written on the right side of the notebook paper.

LaSandra has learned that by giving the students the opportunity to examine, discuss, and identify their need for improvement, they can begin to take more ownership of their work (Andrade et al., 2012). As the students use their notes and other resources to discuss the answers to their tests, they discover where they need to focus their studying. LaSandra has been circulating the room to support on-task behaviors, answer questions, and guide students in their creation of supporting evidence. LaSandra brings the class together to review the correct answers to ensure they have the right information to study. The upcoming test is constructed the same way but with other related questions about the Mayan culture.

By inserting this 15-minute activity into her lesson, she has lead her students to identify items they need to study for the upcoming test and has taken the first steps from giving a standardized, summative assessment to moving toward a more formative approach within her instruction.

The example of LaSandra's class demonstrates how you can shift from a strict, standardized summative approach to incorporating formative processes, but it does not touch on how you can and should meet the variable needs of your students. As discussed in Chapter 2, learners must be recognized as variable if we intend for them to learn and to express what they learn to their fullest. UDL takes the presumptive view that all students can learn, but only when teachers design a learning environment and lessons that can reach all types of student needs by minimizing barriers to learning and expression. To understand why we need to recognize and design for variable learners within the principle of Action and Expression, we turn to the strategic networks.

THE STRATEGIC NETWORKS

When you are planning an action, executing that action, and then monitoring that action, you are using your strategic network (Rose & Meyer, 2002). The strategic networks are extremely complex and are involved in everything we do. From anticipating to assembling, mulling to manufacturing, and yearning to yo-yoing, we each use our strategic networks to take in information, organize it, and do something with it. It doesn't stop there; our strategic networks are what help us monitor what we are doing and make changes based on new or additional information. That information can come from background knowledge or it can be newly introduced information.

Strategic networks are what allow students to piece together and then demonstrate what they know. We must tap into this network to find out how students have connected prior knowledge to new information. It is this network that moves them to becoming the owners, synthesizers, and purveyors of knowledge (Meyer et al., 2013).

THE PRINCIPLE, GUIDELINES, AND CHECKPOINTS

The principle of Action and Expression is equally as rich as the other two principles. Whereas this principle can be quickly related to assessment, this guideline has much more depth (see Figure 5.1). Today's postsecondary opportunities, whether college, the military, or the workforce, all require individuals to identify and accomplish goals. It does not matter what field the person works within or the type of employment, those who can strategize how they will contribute and then make steps toward those contributions are the most effective at their jobs. Students need support and guidance as they mature toward the acquisition of these skills. The guidelines and checkpoints under Action and Expression offer just that by:

- Providing options for executive functions—options to enhance students' abilities around goal setting, planning, managing information, and progress monitoring.

- Providing options for expression and communication—options to support students to communicate information.

- Providing options for physical action—options around physical access to information, tools, and resources.

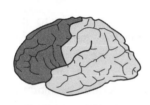

Provide Multiple Means of

Action & Expression

Strategic, goal-directed learners

Provide options for executive functions
+ Guide appropriate goal-setting
+ Support planning and strategy development
+ Enhance capacity for monitoring progress

Provide options for expression and communication
+ Use multiple media for communication
+ Use multiple tools for construction and composition
+ Build fluencies with graduated levels of support for practice and performance

Provide options for physical action
+ Vary the methods for response and navigation
+ Optimize access to tools and assistive technologies

Figure 5.1. CAST's principle of Action and Expression. From Meyer, A., Rose, D.H., & Gordon, D.T. [2013]. *Universal design for learning theory and practice.* Wakefield, MA: National Center on Universal Design for Learning; adapted by permission.

Providing Options for Executive Functions

This guideline focuses on the skills students must build to reach the level of strategic, goal-directed learners (Meyer et al., 2013). When you read the checkpoints, I encourage you to reflect on them in relation to postsecondary environments (e.g., college, trade school, employment, the military). In each case, the stronger students become in the application of the skills under this guideline, the more successful they are likely to be in postsecondary settings.

Guide Appropriate Goal Setting

Goal setting is revered as a skill of successful people and is a focus within our society, but it takes practice and guidance. First, the student needs to want to achieve the goal. Strongly linked to the principle of Engagement, unless the student desires a specific outcome, the creation of a goal will not make a difference. When students want to achieve something, we must help them define what they want to achieve and the steps they will need to take to get there. This will likely involve some scaffolding and modeling. Students can learn about goal setting by creating class-wide goals that also encompass individual goals, as they do in the following scenario.

One Monday afternoon, Valerie's third-grade students became very motivated by the principal's announcement that the third-grade class with the highest number of pages read in level-appropriate books over the course of a month would earn a pizza party. Students had to keep track of the pages they read and talk about those pages with an adult or write about them in their digital or spiral-bound journals. They had three questions to answer each time: What characters were involved in the pages you read? What did those characters do? What do you think they will do next?

While Valerie knew that her students wanted that pizza party, she knew they would need supports to achieve their goal. First, her students helped write a letter to go home to their parents about the challenge, asking parents to support their children in reading level-appropriate books at home and helping their children keep track of the number of pages read. Next, each student estimated the number of pages they normally read while at school and at home. Valerie created what she called the Book Bars Sheet (see Figure 5.2). It was a sheet with vertical bar graphs

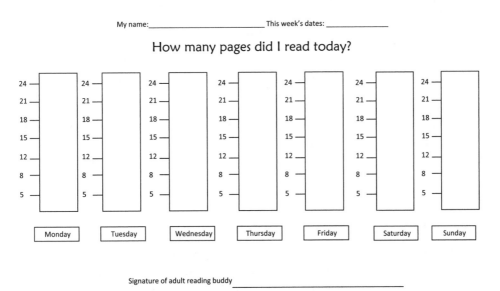

Figure 5.2. Book bars sheet.

for each day of the week (beginning with Monday, ending with Sunday) along with numbers written on the sides, the days of the week written underneath each bar, and a line underneath for the initials of adults. The children wrote the dates under each bar. They then colored the bar on Monday up to the number of pages they estimated that they read. They then discussed what a reasonable goal would be for the number of pages read each day for the remainder of the week. Some students cried out, "20!" while others said, "No! That's too many." It was the perfect entrance into a discussion about individuality and the meaning of *reasonable*. Students then wrote their individual goal for the number of pages they would read at the top of the page.

At the end of the day on Tuesday, they shaded in their Tuesday bar with the number of pages they had read that day and completed the answer to their three questions. Valerie set up response stations in her room with digital recorders for students who wanted to report verbally. Students were used to putting on a head set, pressing record, and following the posted directions that read, "Say your name, say the date, say the name of the assignment, read each question, followed by your answer. When you're done, press stop."

Some of her students left their bar graphs at school because they did not do well with managing papers. She privately asked those students to bring back the parent letter signed so she could be sure those parents knew about the activity. Each morning she posted on the board and verbally reminded students to update their Book Bars Sheet with pages read the night before and to fill in their journals.

At the beginning of the following week, Valerie asked her students to pull out their bar graphs. They looked on their own pages to see if their number of pages had stayed the same, decreased, or increased, and they totaled the number of pages. The students, who were already motivated by the dream of a pizza party, were provided a system to see their progress toward the goal. Valerie totaled the number of pages read by all of her students and shaded in that amount on a class-wide circle graph that looked like a pizza.

For the students in her classroom who were struggling readers, she made sure they and their parents had a list of appropriate books. The principal's goal of the challenge was for students to read pages in level-appropriate books and to get the students talking or writing about what they read. Valerie's added goal was for her students to grow in their ability to set, meet, and possibly exceed their personal goals. The use of an individual student goal sheet for a larger class goal and the breaking down of the larger goal into shorter segments with identified objects is a reflection of the next checkpoint.

In this story, Valerie created a literal way for students to see whether or not they were moving toward accomplishing their goal. They interacted with the bar graphs, had class-wide discussions, and could see how their participation moved the class forward. As individuals, they were also able to see how they connected with the classes' larger goal.

Support Planning and Strategy Development

This checkpoint encourages the use of prompts, coaches, and mentors to support your students as they plan and strategize within lessons. Students need consistent, small, and meaningful reminders to help them plan and strategize. Whether this is a verbal reminder to check the board when they come into the room, a sheet laying out the steps to a process (as in the example about Valerie's response stations), or a completion guide for a project (e.g., a rubric, checklist), these supports should be designed to build your students' levels of independence. Supporting their work within time limits is another example and is discussed later in this chapter. Ultimately, students should become their own monitors and should be using the devices they find to be most helpful to them.

> **PROMOTING EXECUTIVE FUNCTIONS: LAURIE MARTIN AND QUALITY PRODUCT** Laurie Martin uses rubrics and other tools to help her eighth-grade students remain on task, especially when the project takes place over several days. She recognizes, though, that this age group often needs both verbal and written structures if she's going to get the quality product she's seeking. She begins each class revisiting the rubric to ensure the students have followed through with specific steps. This helps them walk through the project successfully. She also emphasizes partner reviews. While the students might think her selection of partners is random, she thoughtfully considers which students provide the strongest feedback to another. This also relates back to the social-emotional needs of her students. Laurie knows she needs to provide a firm structure from which the students can work when providing feedback to one another; otherwise, they can become distracted from the task and more interested in socializing and the selection process she goes through to create those teams.

Dave's students came to appreciate the use of kitchen timers as a device to assess their use of time during his theater class. When the students were working on individual or group activities, Dave would announce the activity goal and then set the timer. When the timer went off, he always asked, "How do you feel about what you accomplished during that time? Is there anything you'll do differently next time to get closer to your goal?" Sometimes they discussed their answers, but he also used those questions to prompt private reflection.

Just as Dave did in the previous example, anytime you slow down the students to let them think about what they are doing, consider next steps, read their next steps, or listen to prompts about next steps, you are putting this checkpoint into action.

Facilitate Managing Information and Resources

Students are inundated with information and resources (i.e., books, digital tools, mechanical or scientific tools) every day, and it can be overwhelming at times. Helping students organize all of that information is important. That can take the form of templates, graphic organizers, charts, or you can give them verbal guidance. Because content-specific environments, specifically in the secondary setting, rely heavily on content lectures, students are placed in a position where note taking is important. It is not surprising that many of these students need support in identifying and noting relevant information (Boyle, 2011). This checkpoint suggests the use of structures for note taking.

One structure is the two-column learning log. The student divides his or her paper vertically with a line. The student then writes the facts from the lecture or text in the left column and in the right column writes why those facts are relevant. The notes from a video about the water cycle might include the fact the water cycle sends water from oceans, lakes, and streams into the atmosphere. The evaporated water turns into clouds and those clouds create rain, which comes back down to the earth.

The student could be provided with a visual diagram of the process and then draw that diagram on the left side of the note page. The student then looks at that information and begins to ask questions, such as, "Does it rain only where there is water on the earth?" "What about deserts?" "What keeps it from raining in places where there is water?" "My mom has a terrarium. Is that like the water cycle?" This strategy not only structures the note-taking process but it also encourages students to delve more deeply into the information. It also encourages students to focus on the ever-important ability to ask questions rather than focus on the assumption that they should always seek the correct and final answer.

Another method includes the cloze method (i.e., leaving certain words or phrases blank on the page and having students fill in that information based on the lecture or reading). To scaffold that strategy further would be to add a word bank at the top of the page. Further scaffolding would involve grouping the word bank according to sections within the notes.

Enhance Capacity for Monitoring Progress

All tasks require us to monitor what we're doing within a process. Whether we're doing something we don't enjoy or something we enjoy immensely, we have to monitor what we're doing. If anything, we monitor where we are in the process of doing to see how soon it will be over (e.g., watching the clock), but we want our students to move beyond clock watching and into the place of reflection. A place where they can clearly identify their strengths and needs related to the current process and seek specific feedback for those strengths or needs. Unless students have come from an environment that fosters this level of self-monitoring, they will need structures and supports to move forward.

It helps when students can visually see their progress on a chart or graph. Any options that exemplify before-and-after status can help students understand their progression within a process. In the example of Valerie's classroom, her use of the bar graph responds to this checkpoint because she draws her students' attention to their achievement or needs. The bar graph in and of itself is not enough, however and the bar graph doesn't address the quality of the students' work. If you recall, there were three questions the students needed to address. Valerie would need to strategize how she would use that information to provide quality feedback to her students so they could use it for self-assessment.

Providing Options for Expression and Communication

This guideline instructs us to consider all of the ways students can communicate to us what they know. When we allow students only one way to demonstrate their knowledge, we risk not realizing what they have learned and what gaps may still exist.

Use Multiple Media for Communication

When asking students to compose something, we tend to turn to the writing of a story or maybe a project that involves paper, scissors, glue, magazine pages, or other such items. This checkpoint encourages us to move into other realms. When students are set free to compose in whatever medium is available to them, it is amazing what they create. This checkpoint includes the platforms students would use to show their work, from hand-drawn cartoons and storyboards to the digital world of blogging and discussion forums.

Beyond composing, this checkpoint also encourages the use of multiple strategies to solve problems. Allowing students to come at problems in their own way, whether real life or instructionally structured, opens the door for rich discussion and self-assessment that connects to the guideline "provide options for self-regulation," under the principle of Engagement, and the guideline "optimize relevance, value, and authenticity." In each case, you are designing an opportunity for students to problem solve around meaningful issues and in ways that make sense to them developmentally. As they experience the difficulties of their approach, they can then reflect on why they might want to hold their path or alter their approach next time.

Use Multiple Tools for Construction and Composition

All students occasionally need supports when composing. Our minds go straight to spellcheckers and even word-prediction software (i.e., the software that guesses what word you're typing on your smart phone, tablet, or computer). Other digital options include everything from text-to-speech software to graphic calculators and music composition software to computer-assisted-design software. If the device can assist students in getting ideas from their heads and onto the paper, screen, or other platform, then it would be included under this checkpoint.

This checkpoint also addresses ways to help students start their compositions. My fourth-grade teacher gave us what she called "story strips." Otherwise known as sentence starters, they helped us begin writing. Using the sentence starters, we could write any story we wanted to as long as we used the vocabulary words correctly (and we couldn't simply copy the definition from the classroom set of dictionaries). We pulled the sentence starters from a hat, which felt invigorating in an otherwise regimented environment. The next part was probably my favorite. She divided us into pairs, and we wrote down the other person's story and read it back to them. As partners, we were responsible for asking questions about the other person's use of the vocabulary words, and we could ask about the story line. This example aligns nicely with this checkpoint but also links with the Engagement guideline "provide options for sustaining effort and persistence."

Build Fluencies with Graduated Levels of Support for Practice and Performance

The principle of Action and Expression doesn't focus just on assessments; it also provides guidance when you're developing activities for practice. When students experience success while practicing their use and application of knowledge, their academic performance outcomes are directly impacted (Bandura, 1997; Usher & Pajares, 2006). Identified as self-efficacy, when students are confident in their academic capabilities they are known to "work harder, evaluate their progress more frequently, and engage in more self-regulatory strategies that promote success" (Usher & Pajares, 2006, p. 7). These outcomes are all in alignment with the ultimate goals of Action and Expression—strategic and goal-directed learners (Meyer et al., 2013).

When you provide students with a multitude of ways to demonstrate their knowledge about a topic or concept, they grow in their ownership of the information. Through scaffolded practice; the guidance of various mentors, guests, or models; mastery-oriented feedback; and the connection to authentic or new-to-them situations, students have the opportunity to move toward the goal as they did in Brandon's classroom, shown in the following example.

Brandon's middle school students were accustomed to working in collaborative groups and teams. They were also used to working with different students within the class. When they were in the midst of working on a lesson on social ethics the students were put into small groups, but each group also had a visitor from the community. Brandon had invited a police officer, a counselor, a psychiatrist, a social worker, a civil attorney, and the executive director of the local homeless shelter. The day before, the students had outlined issues around ethical decision making related to fairness and respect as they related to specific scenarios. They prepared specific questions for the guests, not knowing to whom they would be speaking or that person's profession.

These guests provided the students with real-life connections to the outlined issues. Following the group discussions, Brandon conducted a review in which the groups summarized the assumptions they had prior to their conversations and what new information they had learned. They then revisited a social ethic model Brandon had used to introduce the topic the day before, investigating how what they had learned that day fit within that model.

Brandon offered his students an opportunity to practice using the concepts of social ethics. Through group discussions, statements from the visitors, the review, and revisiting the social ethics model, students practiced with and enhanced their knowledge about an abstract subject. This practice helped them connect to the information and become more confident in their knowledge of the topic.

Provide Options for Physical Action

Within the guidelines of UDL, physical action guides us to think about the options we provide to students so they can express their knowledge. Some students require physical tools due to a disability (e.g., switches instead of a mouse to control a piece of technology), and other students can use technologies to enhance their participation in discussions (e.g., student-response systems). This guideline targets requirements we place on students concerning

- time given for the completion of tasks

- how they respond to information

- how they participate or respond

Vary the Methods for Response and Navigation

The term *navigation* within this checkpoint deals with what options students are provided to respond (e.g., does it have to be with pen or can they use another tool such as a computer, a tape recorder, or some other manipulative to share the same information) and options for time requirements (e.g., do they only have 10 minutes or can they be given additional time).

For example, Beatrice creates a Tic-Tac-Toe strategy of assignments that her seventh-grade students could consider when studying earthquakes. One of the options is to create a poster demonstrating why the lithospheric plates move and what changes they create on Earth. She originally designed the assignment using a 42-inch by 48-inch poster board, but in looking at her lesson design she notes that the size of the poster has nothing to do with the goal. She revises the lesson to include a rubric that shows necessary information to be included and allowed her students to choose how they want to present visually that information.

Digitally, this checkpoint considers the additional hardware some students might need to use a computer or other digital device (e.g., keyboard, adapted keyboard, single switch, joystick). Ultimately, you are ensuring that all students in your classroom have the opportunity to respond to and/or move through the information.

Optimize Access to Tools and Assistive Technologies

This is the only checkpoint that deals directly with technology. It suggests you determine if students need alternatives for their hardware (e.g., mouse, keyboard, customization of a touchpad screen), and to consider the interface between additional hardware and the software used. For students with disabilities, consult their teacher of record. You can also talk directly with the student's parents about devices or tools the student already uses or whether other alternatives are needed. Other students might find that some universal supports help them remain focused on the lesson or task. In an environment designed using UDL, these are the types of supports provided to offer access to all students.

CONCLUSION

The principle of Action and Expression focuses on giving students the opportunity to show what they know. The checkpoints provide specific examples of how you can bridge any possible gaps between what the students know and what they are demonstrating. When students are given options to choose the ways they can show their knowledge, they are more likely to participate in the assessment or assignment.

You can start with choices and options when they do homework. You will see that they will start doing homework when you give them the choice. Chances are they are going to pick something and do it. Then the dynamics of the classroom will change.

—Kandice Castillo, teacher, elementary school

Revisiting Anthony's Lesson

Anthony's lesson was about adding integers. Because this was the first day of the topic, he found a short cartoon video in which the characters were numbers and talked about what it meant to be an integer. It showed them sitting on a number line and how they combined through addition. He gave each student a number line to use and keep in his or her folder and then followed up with a worksheet. Students worked independently, and he went to their desks if they had questions.

This sounds like a UDL lesson, doesn't it? Anthony used a cartoon video, so the students must have been engaged. Add that to the number lines at their desks, and he must have been representing the information to them. They then worked on a worksheet. That's expression, right? This must be a UDL lesson!

Let's interview Anthony about this lesson.

Loui: "Hi Anthony. Thanks for answering some questions about your lesson."

Anthony: "Sure thing!"

Loui: "I'm curious why you chose that video."

Anthony: "We all know kids love the cartoon videos, and I thought the cartoon did a great job of introducing integers."

Loui: "It did look like they enjoyed it. Now, you followed that up with some additional instruction, and then the students worked on their worksheets. Can you tell me why you chose those activities?"

Anthony: "Well, I always follow a video with some lecture. Otherwise, I'm not teaching, right? The students have to hear and see me teach or else I'm not doing my job. Then, I wanted to see if they were getting it, so I gave them the worksheets. I needed some more scores for the grade book, and those need to be individual scores. This way, I can show where they started and then how much growth they have achieved in the next two days as we work on integers. I can't get those scores from group work because that's not fair to all of the students."

Reflect Using the Principle of Action and Expression

Anthony's students had one opportunity to demonstrate their knowledge during the lesson. He "wanted to see if they were getting it," so he provided them with a worksheet. Returning to the discussion on formative and summative assessments, this standardized worksheet (assuming that all of his students received the same worksheet) did not provide any flexibility for his students.

The use of worksheets is still prevalent in our classrooms, but there are other ways for students to practice the acquisition of knowledge. Because this is the first day of integers, taking a grade would only frustrate some students. If it is necessary to take a grade to demonstrate improvement over the course of the unit, make sure students understand the purpose of the assignment and you recognize that there is a strong link between emotion (e.g. how the students are feeling as they enter the assessment) and cognitive performance (i.e., the assessment) (Immordino-Yang, 2007). Having them work in pairs and playing an integer game (e.g., draw a card with an integer written on it, identify where it goes on the number line) to build confidence and knowledge is a great first step. They can support one another's knowledge before they play other teams later. For students who still struggle with the concept of the number line, you can highlight the negative end and the negative sign on the cards. This provided options for comprehension, a guideline under Representation. If students have trouble conceptualizing the number order, have them think about a parking space. When the car is parked in the space, it is at zero. If it backs up, the number of feet it backs away increases. Those are the negative numbers. If it pulls forward, the number of feet also increases. Those are the positive numbers (provide options for comprehension). If there are score sheets or other data collection sheets, Anthony can still collect formative assessment information.

If Anthony feels compelled to use that worksheet, he can have the students work in pairs or small groups to complete the worksheet. By adding the task of each group designing a story problem using integers, he is tapping into their deeper knowledge of the information. For added interest, he can tell the students that he will take the best story problems and use them for upcoming assignments, quizzes, or tests. As he moves around the room, he can gain an initial assessment of their understanding and use that information to shape the next day's lesson. Their homework can include designing two more story problems using integers. This allows Anthony to gather individual assessment information.

Anthony's use of the guidelines under Action and Expression will create more opportunities for students to demonstrate what they have learned and how they can use it. Students can learn how to structure their own time and learning, but only when they are given the chance to try those skills. How you structure your learning environment and lessons will shape all of these potential opportunities.

III

FROM PLANNING
TO PRACTICE

With UDL, teachers design lessons that are purposefully rigorous, relevant, and provide choice and variety. This leads to happy kids who are happy to be there and who are getting it.

—Libby Arthur, social studies teacher and department chair, high school

When I visited Libby's classroom I noticed three things. The goal for the lesson was written on the board, the agenda for the period was written on the board, and all of the students were working in small groups. They were sharing what they already knew about the Revolutionary War and collaboratively defining the vocabulary they would need to know by the end of the unit. Some were writing this information into their notebooks while a few were working around one of the two classroom computers. They were doing the same activity, but they were typing their answers into a document. By the end of the period, each group had determined their roles and work schedules for the upcoming project.

I returned to the same classroom the next day to find the same goal on the board, a new agenda, and to see the students reading. They weren't necessarily reading alone, however. Some were reading their trade books independently. Others were listening to the book through headphones plugged into the same iPod. Two were listening to the book through the computer so they could see the words highlighted at the same time, while a few others were in a small circle reading the book aloud to one another. I noticed that two of the students did not read aloud, but they were a part of the group. This lasted for 20 minutes, and then the students returned to their small groups where they updated their vocabulary and began planning their project plans, which had been introduced at the beginning of the class.

What struck me most was that these two different days were structured completely differently. The continuous piece was the goal. What supported their learning was the environment. Interlaced within these two were the design of the lesson, the guiding agenda, and the variety of resources to which the students had access. These three components came together and allowed Libby to create such an invigorating and productive environment.

Universal design for learning (UDL) is inherently about design, and that is what this section addresses—the materials you have on hand to design your space and what goes on inside of that space. Chapter 6 addresses the materials or resources you have available to you. You are encouraged to think about what you already own and how you use it. Can those uses be expanded to meet the needs of even more students? The chapter then moves into a more thorough discussion about the learning environment.

Chapter 7 begins with the topic of goal writing. This is given attention because the goal is what drives your lesson and the outcomes you've identified for your students. By clarifying your goal you can more efficiently and effectively provide a streamlined lesson. Once you have that goal, you can begin to plan your lesson.

Because there are plenty of lesson-planning formats, this book focuses on the essential pieces of a lesson, why they are important, and some lesson setbacks that can be addressed while planning. For those who prefer to have a lesson plan design within which to work, I discuss CAST's UDL Exchange and, specifically, the lesson plan design tool.

This section concludes the book, bringing together the knowledge you've gained about the framework, the principles, guidelines and checkpoints, and how UDL can be used to enhance or improve your practice. The question "How will I know I'm doing it?" is shifted to "How will I know I'm using UDL to its fullest?" Because there is no tool that can measure whether or not you're designing a UDL lesson or putting that lesson into practice in a "UDL way," I have included seven reflective questions you can ask yourself and others in your teaching community as you design your lessons using the UDL framework.

6

DESIGNING WITH LEARNING IN MIND

I have all of these books and files full of information, and I used to get lost in all of that stuff. Now, I think about what I have and what I want to use. I go by unit and I use the framework to think about how I want the students to experience it, how I want to represent it, and how they are going to show me what they know.
—Kathy Denniston, fifth-grade teacher

Knowing what resources are at your fingertips can open up options and opportunities whether you are designing your environment, lesson, or considering adding other resources to your collection. For the best learning to take place the learning environment needs to be designed so all students have access to learning. The term *learning environment* defines the space where learning takes place, and that space is organized and constructed using available tools, resources, and strategies. Together, these ground the implementation of universal design for learning (UDL). Since barriers to learning can be due to the environment, and your learning environment and lessons will only be as rich as the tools, resources, and strategies you tap, we will look at your space and how it is organized as a design issue.

If you want to light up a room, you purchase a lamp. You decide where it will be positioned in the room, what the style will be, and the amount of light you will need it to provide. For the lamp to work, though, you have to choose the right light bulb. The wrong bulb could damage the shade due to too much heat or give out too little light for your space. The right bulb in the right lamp, however, can create an inviting and workable environment.

Just as your design decisions ensure the lamp and the light bulb partner well, design decisions ensure the creation of a learning environment designed with access and through the selection and use of tools, strategies, and resources. Both require that the other be chosen wisely to meet the need. Because the tools, resources, and strategies are what add to or take away from the learning environment, it's important for you to know what is in your design center.

KNOWING WHAT IS AVAILABLE

For the next few minutes, consider your food pantry at home. When is the last time you took stock of what is in there? Some of you are ultraorganized, but most of us are probably not. Whether your pantry is in a single location or whether your non-perishables are spread throughout the kitchen, you probably don't remember what you have. Things get shoved into the corners, gather dust, and are forgotten. Cans of beans, bags of marshmallows, and boxes of pasta seem to live indefinite lives in these shadowed spots. They are uncovered when you decide to paint, reorganize the kitchen, or search for that sweet or salty snack you're craving. When you find that forgotten item, however, ideas come into your head about the dish you can prepare. You have broadened your choices and options.

Knowing what resources are in your classroom is even more valuable. If you've been teaching for some time, you likely have books, binders, and files full of old lesson plans. Ideas, conference materials, articles, and games are stuck in drawers, cabinets, and lay behind trade books on the back bookshelf. Even if you are new to teaching, you have course materials and curricular supports you received during your courses. Similar to the kitchen pantry, these things don't surface again until you move classrooms or have to pack things for summer construction, but once you find them, they can represent a gold mine.

Building on an action called resource mapping (Center for Mental Health, 2006), figuring out what you have and what you have access to will provide you with options. Resource mapping is typically performed at the school or district level. Over time, a group of people identify what resources (i.e., money, people, programs, services, and facilities) are currently used, and they list or map out how those resources are being used. Based on the identified need, they decide if they need to change how a certain resource is being used, whether the purpose behind a certain resource has ended, or whether new resources need to be identified. In the classroom, you have tools, resources, and strategies. For now, I'm going to group all of them together and call them resources.

If you take stock of your own resources, you can consider new options for your teaching environment and your lessons. Within your learning environment, your identified need is consistent and persistent accessibility. Within lesson planning, your identified need is your goal. Your mapping takes place when you design your environment and lessons, and don't forget that your resources might include people (e.g., visiting experts), digital devices owned by the students, and those little desk clerk bells you purchased for last years' game-show activity.

The format you use to list your resources will depend on how you make decisions, what grade level you teach, and what subject you teach. Also, this is something that will take time—maybe even up to a year. Give yourself that freedom. The goal of this activity is to know what you have so you can use it in the design of your learning environment and lessons.

When it comes to listing what you have, you can get as specific or as broad as you like. Some of you will go as far as listing titles of books and articles, labeling binders, and grouping like items together (e.g., math manipulatives will now be stored in the same plastic container in the back cabinet, curricular materials that directly address the trade books you use are now grouped together, music scores are now sorted alphabetically by composer), but others of you don't operate that way. Things are spread about your room and fit the way you think and teach. Either way is fine, and no way is better than another. Since this book is about UDL, and we all vary in the ways we operate, this section on resource mapping provides you with suggestions on how to identify and manage your tools, resources, and strategies (i.e., you are managing your own information and resources, which is a checkpoint under Action and Expression). You ultimately choose the best way to organize and reference your resources.

Figures 6.1, 6.2, and 6.3 show three forms that provide some ideas on how you might identify what you own and where you keep it. Again, I emphasize that how you identify and organize your resources is your own preference. You might not agree

	English/ language arts	Math	Science	Social studies	Health	Recess	Location specific (e.g., reading rug)
Conference materials							
Books about teaching strategies							
Personally owned software							
Things that plug in or require a battery							
Subject specific manipulatives							
Student-owned technology							
Other resources							

Figure 6.1. Elementary mapping

	Subject/ period	Subject/ period	Subject/ period	Subject/ period	Subject/ period	Subject/ period	Subject/ period
Conference materials							
Books about teaching strategies							
Personally owned software							
Stuff that plugs in or requires a battery							
Subject specific manipulatives							
Student-owned technology							
Other resources							

Figure 6.2. Middle school/high school mapping

Suggested item		Your item	Location in classroom
Conference materials			
	Specific topic:		
	Specific strategy:		
Teaching books			
	Specific topic:		
	Specific strategy:		
Personally owned software			
	Specific topic:		
Stuff that plugs in or requires a battery			
	Audio (e.g., tape recorder)		
	Visual (e.g., overhead)		
	Tablet		
	Laptop		
	Calculators		
	Other		
Subject-specific manipulatives			
	1.		
	2.		
	3.		
Student-owned technology			
	1.		
	2.		
	3.		
Web-based resources			Favorites folder/drive/ USB
	Name		
	Name		
	Name		
	Name		

Figure 6.3. Classroom mapping

with the design or the grouping of items. You might find that it is easier to list things on a single sheet of paper. You might create a new file system. You might not need to write anything down because once you've located it, you won't forget it. This exercise is about you knowing what you have so you can begin to think of 1) whether the originally defined use or the resources create a barrier for learners and 2) the different ways the resources can be used.

Having a clear sense of the tools and resources you have on hand and knowing the types of strategies you prefer informs the design of your learning environment.

If you are currently teaching, you already have an established learning environment. You'll be looking to see if you should refine or change anything. If you are not currently teaching, then you will be creating that environment in your head. Notice that I did not say "perfect environment." This is because there is no perfect environment. Perfect implies finished, and the implementation of UDL is never finished. This goes back to the concept of variable learners, which I wrote about in Chapter 2. While some things remain in place (e.g., stations, certain wall posters, the placement of the classroom computers), *how* you ask your students to use them and *why* they use them will change.

What About Adopted Materials?

Many classroom teachers, especially those in the general education setting, have curricular materials that are adopted by their department, grade level, or team. These materials often come in the form of a textbook with accompanying materials. These prepared curricula come with ingrained structures and values from historical, social, and cultural contexts that cause them to ignore alternative ideas or provide relevant representations of current and historical people, places, activities, and events. They can lean toward or away from certain concepts or pedagogical methods, and many are not in line with reform-based standards or practices (Beyer & Davis, 2011).

Each of these dimensions affects how you deliver the curriculum (Cohen & Ball, 1999). You also use your own beliefs, experiences, and knowledge to interpret these materials (Beyer & Davis, 2011; Brown, 2009; Remillard, 2005). Add to this the plethora of resources discussed previously, and the relationship between you and the adopted materials shifts. Because you can enhance, broaden, and deepen the adopted materials, that relationship becomes collaborative versus prescriptive (Beyer & Davis, 2011). That collaborative relationship is the premise to your use of the UDL framework.

Teachers were once viewed as a mere conduit of delivery; now, teachers are recognized as active decision makers, planners, and designers. Even if you are in a setting that requires you follow a specific curriculum in a specific way, you can enhance that curriculum by incorporating other resources. This focuses on the *how* of choosing resources and the design of your learning environment.

If you have had the opportunity to visit the classrooms of other teachers when there are students present, you have seen the variety of environments out there. We can't help but have our learning preferences exemplified in our environments, but it's our job to move beyond that because we know that not every student learns the way we do. Once we step outside of our personal structures, the world of learning can open up for our students.

THE LEARNING ENVIRONMENT

You have to create the learning environment first. Once you have that, your lessons will work within it. The learning environment is what lets you meet each lesson's goal.

—George Van Horn, Director of Special Education

In Chapter 2 I defined the learning environment to include the physical location where learning is taking place, the resources available to the students, and the design of the lesson. To add a little more clarity, consider a widely used analogy—the buffet.

Pretend you are at the perfect buffet. The price is right, the food is fresh, it tastes delicious, and the restaurant is filled with happy people. The chairs and booths are comfortable, there's plenty of room between tables to get back and forth from the buffet, the staff are welcoming, and the environment feels inviting. Although there are some foods there that you don't like, there are plenty of foods you do like. Some of the choices are hot and some are cold. There are simple foods, such as carrots and lettuce, and other combined foods, such as macaroni and cheese or gelatin with marshmallows. Whether you're a vegan, a vegetarian, a carnivore, or anything in between, you find plenty of food to satisfy your palate.

You are able to choose which foods you like and skip the ones you don't like. You know your health goals, so you can make informed choices about single or second helpings. You also know if you have allergies or sensitivities to certain foods, so you stay away from the ones you know about and you ask the servers to clarify the ingredients of others. Because it is a buffet, you can come at different times during the day or week and know that this experience and your favorite foods will be there.

The buffet analogy demonstrates access and the issues of personal goal setting and decision making. More important, the buffet analogy demonstrates a quality learning environment because it provides the same variety of options and supports in this same way, every day. These are not modifications or accommodations that are made according to the food served or the patrons buying the food. The buffet is designed this way so that every customer who walks in will have the best experience possible and will want to return. The next step is translating this into your classroom, which I have broken down into three components: fitting in, choice, and getting to what you need.

Fitting In

Fitting in relates to the affective networks, thus, the principle of Engagement. When you fit in, you are interested in being where you are, you enjoy being where you are, and you want to contribute. Because you can fully participate in the present activity, you want to be there. You gauge your own involvement, noticing when you're not on task and what will help you stick with your goals or keep you interested. Feeling that you fit within an environment sets you up to learn; your brain is ready to go (Rose & Meyer, 2002).

Discussed more in Chapter 3, the affective networks negotiate how students interpret what they are experiencing or learning. Their ability to learn is directly influenced by their own emotions, needs, and memories (Rose & Meyer, 2002). This is why it is so important to pay close attention to the design of the learning environment in relation to the affective network.

Returning to the buffet example, your favorite foods are there, and that food is fresh and deliciously prepared. You are there because you are hungry, but the quality of the food and the restaurant atmosphere definitely influence whether or not you will stay. If the restaurant didn't meet your requirements for quality of food, cleanliness, noise level, and staff friendliness and attentiveness, you would probably leave. There is one part of any buffet, however, that could be problem.

You have all of this food in front of you, and you get to consume all that you want. What if you have health concerns? Maybe you have dietary restrictions on caloric intake, or allergies, or sensitivities to certain foods, or you know that too much of a certain type of food will give you a stomachache (even if you love the taste of it). You have to use your own intrinsic drivers to guide you. When you are at a buffet, you have to make choices based on the information you already know, are willing to access, and/or understand how to access (e.g., asking a staff person for a nutrition chart or a list of ingredients). The more positive choices you make about your own health, the more empowered you are to create a healthy body.

Let's say you want to make an empowered choice. Because you know you're going to a buffet, this time you invite a close friend who supports your dietary goals and will serve as an excellent influencer each time you fill your plate. In a few months' time, you'll probably be able to go to the buffet without the support of that friend because you will have gained a set of skills or internal drivers that will help you make the right decisions, even when the wrong one is right in front of you.

The previous example gets to the anticipated outcome connected to the principle of Engagement. When you design the learning environment so that students are provided the opportunity to fit within an environment, they gain an understanding of self-regulation through scaffolded practice and support (see Figure 6.4).

Scaffolding is the term used for temporary supports that help students when they initially acquire a new skill. The most important word in that previous sentence is *temporary*. If the scaffold becomes long term or permanent, then the learner becomes reliant on it and will not improve his or her acquisition of the skill. However, you cannot take away the scaffolding too soon or the students' skills will not improve.

Kandice's Story

I think that as you're teaching you quickly find out what students are able to give you about what they will give to you. In utopia, you would say, "Here's your project" and they do it, but it's never really been that way.

I gave my students an assignment of a book report at the beginning of the 9 weeks, and it was due at the end of the 9 weeks. The big goal was for them to successfully read a level-appropriate book and share information about that book in a way that let me know they understood the content. I gave them a variety of choices for their book reports, and we conferenced to make sure each student understood the assignment and chose an appropriate book (see Figure 6.1).

There was time provided for independent reading, or they could use down time, but they also needed to read at home. Knowing one of my students,

(continued)

(continued)

I knew that was not going to happen at home and that he wouldn't get the reading done in school, either. I teamed up with another teacher, and she was able to tape herself reading his book. When everyone else was doing independent reading, he was able to independently listen to the tape, so he was still getting the content. Even though the book was still on his level, knowing him he would have never finished the book or the project. I decided that this was the scaffolding he needed to be successful to accomplish the big idea.

He still needed guidance with the project part. He wanted to do a diorama. Again, I knew he wouldn't get it done at home and wouldn't have access to the materials. I provided him with a shoe box, construction paper, and then he had to use what he learned from the story to create the diorama. He wanted to focus on ships, so I made sure he had blue, for water. He needed help to get through the book and getting the materials, but it was up to him to take those materials and go from there. I helped guide him a little bit to get him thinking. That was the scaffolding to make him successful.

When the projects were due, the students got to take pride, responsibility, and ownership of their project. They could present if they wanted to or they could pass, but everybody wanted to present what they did. This young man presented his, too.

Book Report

As a conclusion to the first semester of fifth grade, students will complete a report on a book that is on their reading level that they have read during the second nine weeks. The student and teacher will agree on a book that can be read for this project.

Requirements: Student must read a book on their reading level to complete the report. Books should be chosen by November 1, 2012.

Book report is due on December 14, 2012.

Book report is worth 100 points (15% of your reading grade).

*50 points for presentation (neatness, words spelled correctly, title of the book found on the project, project displays information about the book, project demonstrates comprehension of the book read)
*20 points for answering the three essential questions (questions were answered in complete sentences, all three questions were answered)
*10 points for creativity
*10 points for having all requirements met on the project chosen
*5 points for completion
*5 points if book was on reading level

Student must answer the following questions:

1. What book did you read and why?
2. What project did you choose and why?
3. What chapter was your favorite? Explain using page numbers and specific examples from your book.

Each student will create a project representing the book they chose using one of the following choices:

1. Create a bulletin board/poster board to display various events from your book. (Include categories with character names, settings, and the plot of the story.)
2. Create a timeline describing major events in the story. (Include characters and settings from the story.)
3. Create a diorama of one of the major settings in the story. (Include characters in your diorama with key components from the story. Use a shoe box or a small cardboard box.)
4. Create a trivia game to explain the story. (Create a game board with pieces and trivia cards asking questions about the story, characters, setting, etc., with answers on the back.)
5. Create a puppet show to summarize the events from the story. (Create puppets to demonstrate characters from the story. The story line needs to incorporate events from the book, including a backdrop to demonstrate one of the settings from the book.)
6. Create a song or rap to summarize the story from the beginning to the end. (Sing or rap a song explaining the events from the book to include major characters/setting/problem/solution.)
7. Create a mobile to share key components from the book read. (Include characters, setting, and major events from the story.)
8. Create a new book cover for the book. (Include characters, setting, important phrases/events from the book.)
9. Create your own Accelerated Reader test for your book. (Include 20 multiple-choice questions about your book. Three of the choices would be wrong and one choice would be the correct answer.)
10. Write a report about the book that you read. (Report may be handwritten or typed, at least two pages long, and must include the author of the book, characters, setting, plot, problems, and solutions within the book.)

Figure 6.4. Kandice's lesson examples.

Kandice's example provides some precise connections to the framework and demonstrate how her environment is designed to be accessible to the variable learners. There is some overlap with the design of her lesson, but there are key components to her story that demonstrate the flexibility of her environment.

Although this story focused on the needs of one young man, this was not a young man with an identified learning disability. Instead, Kandice decided that this student needed the flexibility of a recorded book versus a text-based book. There was no individualized education plan accommodation suggesting to her that this modification be made. The decision was made based on need and the equal desire for the student to achieve the goal of the unit. He needed a different way to achieve that goal but still to demonstrate the same level of comprehension asked of his peers. This connects back to the principle of Representation and providing options for language, mathematical expressions, and symbols. It also diminished the threat that this young man might have experienced toward the assignment, knowing that he would not complete it. This falls under Engagement and the guideline "provide options for recruiting interest."

Next, she provided time during class for the students to read their trade books. The young man was able to listen to his book during that time. She recognized the needs of her fifth-grade students to have a structure around their executive functions (i.e., goal setting, using their time appropriately, using the resources available to them, and providing them with a tool to monitor their own progress).

Another example is Kandice's use of the conferences. This was her way of checking in with the students to monitor their decisions, ensure they chose a book at their level, and make sure they had the materials necessary for their book reports and could move forward on their projects. Here, too, Kandice employed the principle of Action and Expression as she helped her students build on their executive functions.

Although his peers didn't need the support of verbalized text, this young man was able to function within that environment, knowing that he was equal to his peers. He fit in both academically and socially because he was supported to do so. Kandice provided scaffolding around accessing the print, but did not alter the goal. Just as this young man did, if your students experience that sense of belonging fitting in through social support, they are more likely to internalize the goals set forth and share in your value of education (Dotterer & Lowe, 2011).

Choice

Choice covers all of the brain networks and principles. When students are offered choices in how they connect to their learning (i.e., Engagement and the affective networks), consume knowledge (i.e., Representation and the recognition networks), and demonstrate their knowledge (i.e., Action and Expression and the strategic networks), they are going to be more responsive (Rose & Meyer, 2002). The concept of choice can be difficult for teachers to consider. We begin to think about the number of students we teach and managing the classroom. As you design your environment, you can build in choice. Through the investigation of your own teaching patterns, you see how those patterns might be made more accessible and you put those structures in when you design the learning environment.

For example, you might enjoy using stations in your classroom, but as you compare the design of those learning stations with the UDL framework you might discover that students are experiencing barriers to their learning at your listening station. Let's say that the rule is to listen and not talk. This design creates a barrier for some students. Students who need additional input to understand the story cannot ask questions of their peers. Instead, they have to wait, which causes them to detach from the learning and information. Without changing the basic structure of the station, you could add in a "speak or write your question" rule. Students could have access to a tape recorder and sticky notes so they can speak or write their question on the spot. This way, students can take their questions to a conversation station where they can present their questions for further discussion and debate. This not only supports choice, it also encourages students to think about the story as they are listening to it and participate in student-led discussions.

Returning to the buffet example, the ability to make a choice is crucial to whether or not you will return. The foods are labeled clearly and you can monitor your diet, any potential allergy or sensitivity needs, and you will be sure to choose only the foods you like. If you can't read a sign, one of those friendly staff can explain the food to you. Beyond just choosing the food, though, you get to choose whether or not you want to have seconds, and you choose the foods that fit with your personal diet and nutrition goals. This is analogous to a student choosing what strategy, tool, or resource to use to learn about a topic and the personal goals to use for learning.

Let's look at choice from the perspective of another subject. Although this example is about a specific lesson, think about how the options offered could be woven into the environment and made available during all lessons.

In your algebra class the goal is for the students to demonstrate their understanding of how to multiply two-termed polynomials using the FOIL method (first, outside, inner, last). At this point, students are familiar with integers (i.e., whole numbers that are positive or negative) and two-termed polynomials; for example, $(x + 4)(x + 2)$. You look at the principle of Representation and see that it is important to find many different ways to present and clarify the information while highlighting the present patterns. You also know that while some of your students prefer lecture with examples, there are other students who get lost during your lectures. They need to hear what you're saying multiple times to break it down. For these students, you offer tape recordings of the lecture with the notes written out step by step (another student takes these notes during the lecture). You use colored chalk or markers to represent the different steps of the FOIL method. You remind your students that they can do the same, and you make sure these colors are incorporated into the student note taker's notes. Student mentors are identified to provide additional supportive information. If you have a flip camera and post information on a class web site, you can post the notes there. If students have access to the Internet, they can turn to places like the Kahn Academy. All of this is to demonstrate that choice and supports can be offered simultaneously or across time. Those supports become a buffet from which the students might choose, and when those supports become a natural part of how your classroom runs versus a single-shot support during one lesson, then you are creating an environment designed through the use of UDL.

ACTION AND EXPRESSION: LAURIE MARTIN AND CHOICE THROUGH PROJECTS Laurie Martin recognizes the importance of choice within the context of Action and Expression. This helps her ensure that her eighth-grade students can fully demonstrate their knowledge. By giving them a variety of ways they can demonstrate their knowledge, Laurie creates an environment where the students have to select the method with which they feel most comfortable and confident. Through these actions she is helping them become more strategic in their decision making. She notes, "if I'm telling them, 'you have to do this,' it's not going to be as much fun or it's not going to be as meaningful to them as if they have some choice, so I always like to give them choice."

Getting to What You Need

Getting what you need is another way to talk about access. Defined in Chapter 2, "access can refer to accessible instructional materials (AIM) and flexible resources. Access can also refer to a student simply being able to connect to the information being taught." In this scenario, being able to connect also involves a physical component.

The buffet example mentions that you prefer the space between the tables because you can easily get to and from the buffet. You can reach the foods you want, or one of those friendly staff people will help you. Beyond the physical piece, the price is just right for your budget and you can go back for seconds or even thirds if you want to. That same friendly staff are ready to answer your questions about the food or get you another plate if you need one.

When the learning environment is structured to help students get what they need, you can begin moving them toward the ultimate position of a resourceful, knowledgeable, strategic, goal-setting, purposeful, and motivated learner (Meyer, Rose, & Gordon, 2013). This kind of access creates an environment that is open, inviting, and stimulating. When you disallow this kind of access, students cannot experience growth in these characteristics and will experience a limiting environment.

Research shows a relationship between "students' perceptions of a positive classroom climate, their corresponding engagement in classroom activities, and their academic performance" (Dotterer & Lowe, 2011, p. 1651). This means it is crucial that students sense they can learn within the environment they are experiencing and that they are able to explore learning in ways that suit their learning needs. Referring back to one of the outcome characteristics supported by the UDL framework, students cannot learn to be resourceful unless they know they will be supported as they locate what they need.

For example, you've asked your students to find sources to support their theory about cell division. Your interdisciplinary team is also leading a unit on appropriate Internet use, and this unit is embedded within all of your lessons this month. To build on the desired outcome characteristics of UDL, you have designed a rubric to specify what you'd like to see in relation to the students' sources (i.e., number of sources, quality, and source location). The interdisciplinary team created a rubric on appropriate Internet use, the students received direct instruction and practiced with it, and they have access to the rubric. They also know they can ask questions about how to use an online search engine. By creating these supports and expectations, your students know they fit within the learning environment and they sense and experience access and choice. They are more likely to begin the exploration of resourcefulness.

SELF-REGULATION SKILLS IN MIDDLE SCHOOL: TAMARA LECLERC AND PROMOTING RESOURCEFULNESS   Tamara LeClerc promotes resourcefulness through the design of the teaching environment. She lays out her classroom procedures during the first few days of school and these procedures remain consistent throughout the year. These classroom structures give time back to her for instruction and build on student ownership. As her middle-school students become more independent within the classroom environment, she has more time to provide just-in-time support to those students in need. From posting the day's agenda to maintaining a make-up work center, she maintains the expectation that all of her students mature into thoughtful learners who are able to access the tools and information they need.

The design of your learning environment is your opportunity to create a welcoming, engaging, and stimulating space. Many times we design our rooms based on what we own, what we can purchase at the teacher store, and what our peers have in their rooms. Or maybe we see a picture of a room we find interesting in a magazine or on the Internet. These can all be wonderful points of inspiration, but if you want to create an environment that is truly accessible to all students, use the UDL framework to investigate your purpose behind your design. Doing so will help bring your lesson to life.

CONCLUSION

This chapter began with the concept of resource mapping at the classroom level. What could be seen as a laborious and overwhelming task is one that can open opportunities and options to you as you investigate your learning environment. Returning to the concept of accessibility as a way to reach all learners, knowing what you have and then choosing how and why you use it allows you to more freely plan your lessons. Because your learning environment will now be designed to provide students with real opportunities to learn, you can focus on the specifics of your lessons. In a well-constructed learning environment, you and your students will be prepared to meet your clearly defined learning goals, and they will have more opportunities to achieve their learning outcomes.

7

THE GOAL AND THE LESSON

> If you have a clear sense of what you're going to do each day and for each lesson, you can get a better hold on what universal design for learning (UDL) is because you know what you want to teach. Now, you're figuring out how to teach it.
>
> —Matt Roberts, seventh-grade math teacher

I talked about the lesson goal in Chapter 6 by saying, "The goal is the heart of any lesson. All activities, resources used, and products produced should be grounded in that goal."

By defining what you want to teach, as Matt states, you are set free to use the UDL framework and decide how you're going to construct that lesson. Moreover, if you've worked on the design of your learning environment, you can meet your goal more efficiently.

THE LESSON GOAL

"This book, like any good lesson, has a goal. That goal is to provide the reader with a solid understanding of UDL so that person can develop effective lessons" (Preface, p. xi). Notice that the goal of this book doesn't say how the reader will come to that understanding. That is because goals most effectively used in conjunction with the UDL framework are written with the outcome in mind but do not specify how that outcome will be reached. In other words, the target or purpose (the *what*) of the lesson is stated, but the methods used to reach this (the *how*) are not included (Coyne et al., 2009). By including a defined method, the teacher is limited to that specific strategy or tool, thus ignoring the multitude of resources available, the spontaneous scaffolding that can occur, and the potential for additional enrichment.

What if you are required to include the *how* in your goal? Some school districts, principals, or others require teachers to place the *how* into their goals. By using broad descriptors such as *demonstrate, compose,* or *figure,* teachers leave the door open for the necessary flexibility and choice in a UDL lesson. Table 2.1 in Chapter 2 shows suggested descriptors. Another list is located later in this chapter under the section "Choosing the Right Words."

To more thoroughly discuss goals, the first section of this chapter describes the role of goals, how to design goals using the Common Core State Standards (CCSS) as an example, and closes with a discussion of how goals promote student ownership of learning. First, we begin with a fairy tale.

The King's Path Makers

Once, there was a king who wanted a new path to the river. He called together his kingdom's best path makers and said, "Go out and create the best path possible to the river."

The path makers went back to their workshops, gathered their path-making tools, and began their work. In a month's time they completed their task. One path maker was driven by precision. He used a compass and created the most direct route. Another was driven by beauty. She knew of meadows with blooming flowers along the way and created a meandering, flower-filled path. The third was driven by physical challenge. She knew of steep inclines and deep descents and created a path worthy of mountaineers.

At the end of the month the king called them all together. While waiting for their majesty, a conversation occurred:

"I am sure my path will be preferred by the king because it is the fastest path," said the first path maker.

"Oh, I am sure you are incorrect," said the second. "The king enjoys beautiful things, and he will like nothing better than to see the natural beauty present within his kingdom as he takes his daily walks to the river."

The third disagreed, saying, "You are both wrong. The king is a powerful man who enjoys challenge and strenuous activity. He will choose mine as the best path."

When the king arrived, the matter was settled. "I took time this morning to explore each of your paths, and I thank you for your thoughtfulness, engineering, creativity, and persistence. I am delighted to have three ways to get to and from the river. On days when I am pressed for time and need to return for meetings with my council, I can take the direct path. On days when I am contemplative and want beauty at my side, I can take the winding path. On days when I am agitated or I want to revel in my physical strength, I can take the challenging path.

"But sire, which of us won? Which of us created the best path?" asked the path makers.

"Ah! You see, I asked you to create the best path possible, which each of you did. Using your tools, gifts, and vision you created three very different paths that all take me to the same place. For this I am grateful, as you should be; for now you have discovered that in your differences is a strong similarity. You all achieved the same goal in your own way."

The Role of Goals

The king told his path makers to create the best path possible. In this tale the king created an environment that allowed the path makers to use their individual skills to give him their best work. That's what UDL guides us to do in the classroom.

The primary role of the lesson goal is to offer direction to both the teacher and the students, related to the lesson. Additionally, a well-written goal allows the teacher to analyze the lesson (Hattie, 2009; Jansen et al., 2009). The goal is both the gateway to the lesson and the path to determining the lesson's effectiveness. If you write a well-defined learning goal you can examine the alignment between your instruction and the goal, your students' achievement of the goal, and make the necessary revisions for later use of the lesson (Hattie, 2009; Morris, Hiebert, & Spitzer, 2009). These three pieces are discussed in the next sections.

Alignment

When a car is aligned, it drives along the road smoothly. The wheels are set at the correct angle so the tires wear evenly. It can drive a straight line and not pull in one direction or another, and the tire tread can effectively grip the road. When the lesson is in alignment with the goal, it stays on your defined path. The goal becomes the center line on the road of your lesson.

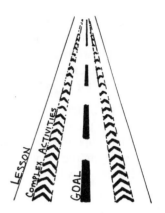

If your activities or assessments pull too far to one side or another, the lesson will not be as effective because it won't be on point. By defining the specific point of the lesson, you can structure in complex activities, push students toward higher order thinking, and know that you are not pulling them away from the ultimate goal. You are guiding your students' learning as you all go down the road together. Stiggens (2008) suggested framing the goal as an "I can ..." statement. This helps the teacher focus on the desired student outcomes and can also support the students in determining their own level of mastery. Through the use of guiding supports and structures, students will have the guidance needed to seek support when they find themselves off target of the specified goal (Jones, Jones, & Vermette, 2011).

Regardless of the strategy you use to tighten your goal, the main point is to guide the instruction you are offering, the work students will do, and the evidence they will provide of their understanding. To offer some examples, Table 7.1 lists goals that identify specific and nonspecific points. Each of the goals are related to a CCSS.

Table 7.1. Developing specific goals

Specific point: Students will choose from a variety of measuring devices to measure the length of different items.

Nonspecific point: Students will learn about measurement.

Common Core State Standard referenced: CCSS.Math.Content.2.MD.A.1

Specific point: Students will recognize pairs of words that rhyme.

Nonspecific point: Students will practice with rhyming words.

Common Core State Standard referenced: CCSS.ELA-Literacy.RF.K.2a

Specific point: Students will combine information gathered from a variety of sources and share that information comprehensively using collaboratively designed options.

Nonspecific point: Students will read from a variety of resources and combine their ideas.

Common Core State Standard referenced: CCSS.ELA-Literacy.SL.6.2

Examining Achievement

When we think of examining student achievement, we tend to think of assessments. Addressed more in Chapter 5, under the principle of Action and Expression, considering any kind of information from students as a way to examine their growth will help you examine your goals. Comparing informal, lesson-related feedback from your students to the goal of the lesson helps you determine the effect you had through your lesson.

- Goal: "Students will calculate the molarity of selected solutions." A quick walk-through of the room shows you that some students are struggling at the same point within the process of calculating the molarity of different solutions. You provide a miniseminar at the side of the room using other approaches and examples for any students who wish to come.

- Goal: "Students will begin their investigation of how diet affects mood." You call out "Pop idea!" which makes the students pull out a piece of paper write down what pops into their head when they think about their mood and food. After scanning the ideas, you see that students are able to use words or figures to articulate how their diet affects their mood.

- Goal: "Student groups will demonstrate the effect of the Peloponnesian War on the political structure of Athens." A miniconference with each workgroup allows you to see where they are within their project, who is completing what task, and who might need further support. A few groups are not demonstrating a depth in their knowledge. You prompt them with additional questions and suggestions to consider during their next work time.

Each of these examples demonstrates the continuous types of informal assessment we conduct. However, the information collected during these informal assessments is only valuable when considered through the lens of your goal. Think of your goal and designed assessments as destined to be married.

If you begin the construction of your lesson by knowing the point of your goal, then your assessments, both formal and informal, will be easier to construct and will provide you with better information (see Table 7.2).

Additional questions you can ask yourself during the design of your lesson include the following:

Top hat: "I promise to tell you exactly what we want students to learn."
Veil: "I promise to tell you whether students have learned what we want them to learn."

- When designing the lesson, ask, "How will I know that my students are meeting the goal?"

- During the lesson, ask, "Are my students demonstrating movement toward the goal?"

- After the lesson, ask, "Did my students meet the goal I determined for this class?"

Table 7.2. The vows

The goal: I promise to teach the students a new topic, skill, or concept.
The assessment: I promise to assess their acquisition of that topic, skill, or concept.

The goal: I promise to expand my students' knowledge about a topic, skill, or concept.
The assessment: I promise to assess their expanded knowledge of that topic, skill, or concept.

The goal: I promise to guide them to use knowledge they have.
The assessment: I promise to assess their ability to transfer and apply that knowledge.

The goal: I promise to shift their position on a topic.
The assessment: I promise to assess the positions they held at the beginning and hold at the end.

In all three phases, and the times in between, attention to the UDL framework can help you create assessments, whether they are informal or formal, formative or summative. For example, things shift during the teaching day. Maybe you don't include a resource you planned on using, the students are particularly distracted today, or you forget to provide them the structured reminders you planned to use to keep them on task. Regardless, you notice that your students are not demonstrating their absorption of the information.

A quick scan of the room tells you that the majority of the students are off task. They were attentive at the beginning of the lesson, but once they began work on their projects, you noticed more off-task behavior. The goal for this unit is, "Students will assemble evidence demonstrating the guilt or innocence of their bacteria in relation to the described infection." For today, you have written, "Students will gather information about their bacteria connected to their guilt or innocence." They have a rubric that further clarifies the unit and today's goal, and you feel really good about the instructions you gave; after all, you used the framework to help you design the rubric and your instructions. You focused on using straightforward language, you used visuals, and you answered questions. You could say, "If I don't see more people working on their projects, you're going to lose your project time." That might curb their behavior temporarily, but if they don't understand the assignment, topic, or goal, they aren't going to connect to the project. So now what? A quick scan under the principle of Representation brings you to the guideline "provide options for comprehension" and the checkpoint "Highlight patterns, critical features, big ideas, and relationships." You then ask volunteers to talk about the goal and requirements of the assignment without looking at the instructions you printed out for them. This is to put the goal and requirements into student-friendly language. This also agrees with the principle of Action and Expression, which reminds you of executive functions. You have clarified what they need to complete that day through the voice of their peers. You list those steps on the board and make sure those steps directly connect to their achievement of the goal.

The framework can help you consider on-the-spot ways to address these types of typical issues. You can also use the framework to seek additional options to add to future lessons. If you do add additional supports, make sure those supports are based on your desired outcomes.

A popular informal strategy used throughout the K–12 grades is exit tickets (Owen & Sarles, 2012). This method is used to check students' understanding and can serve as a scaffold toward developing their own achievement monitoring (Fisher & Frey, 2007). Typically distributed during the last few minutes of class, exit tickets provide an informal structure to create a consistent, feedback-rich environment. Used properly, exit tickets become a time for students to reflect on what they know and to return to a larger project or lesson unit and revise their thinking. Jones and Dotson (2010) believed these types of environments are "essential to reflection."

Tamara uses exit tickets daily at the end of her middle school health class. While they always link to the lesson goal, sometimes they are open-ended questions and other times they are in multiple-choice or true–false format. Her goal today was, "Students will explore the concept of self-esteem." During the lesson, the students were introduced to the definition of self-esteem, did a self-assessment of their strengths and needs in relation to school, other activities, relationships with others, and what they do during their free time using a self-interview guide. They considered what they learned about themselves and created a visual representation of themselves using that information. As a part of her exit ticket, Tamara asked them to choose one of the three definitions of self-esteem posted on the board. They also needed to write down something they learned about their own self-esteem. Students are always permitted to draw pictures versus writing. If she can't figure out what they drew, she interviews them during the next class period. For students who struggle with their handwriting but who like to write, she always has half sheets of paper with lines on them.

Exit tickets can give us the evidence we need to make the necessary improvements to our lessons (Leahy, Lyon, Thompson, & Wiliam, 2005). As one teacher from Colorado commented,

I ask students to share something they figured out from the day's lesson or reading and something they wondered or were confused about. I don't grade this. I simply look for patterns in thinking. While I read, I reflect on how I might tweak my minilesson for the next class. (Tovani, 2012, p. 51)

As long as you structure your exit-ticket questions to reflect the presented goal, you will have information to help you answer whether or not the students truly connected with and learned from the lesson.

Revision

The practice of reflection, addressed in Chapter 3, is important when revising a lesson. This is a time when you examine how well your lesson went. Outside of returning to and reviewing your entire lesson plan, there are some overarching pieces you can consider, including student participation and interaction, the introduction to the lesson, activities, assessments, and scaffolding. Finally, you'll want to investigate whether your goal directed the design and implementation of the pieces mentioned.

The lesson-reflection time brings to life interesting intrapersonal considerations. When we look at our lesson outcomes, it is easy to see the student behavior as the driver—but what if we alter that perspective and see how our lessons are an equal driver in creating learning outcomes? For example, beginning a lesson by clearly identifying and building on our students' background knowledge ensures they are prepared to learn and they are connected to the topic. Because you know the goal of the lesson, you can truly construct this piece to meet the variable needs of your students. You use this same information to design your activities and assessments.

Looking back at the scaffolding you provided will often offer you some rich information. When students lose interest it can be because they don't understand some component of the lesson. Teasing this out is crucial, and your students are your best resource.

Rhonda Laswell, a former seventh-grade science teacher and current UDL coordinator, agrees, saying, "Our students give us our best information. If we just listen to them, we find out what they need." All of this information goes into the revision of the lesson. The act of revision is practiced by master teachers and is known to be a significant component to creating an effective learning environment (Hiebert, Morris, Berk, & Jansen, 2007).

Returning to the lamp and light bulb analogy in Chapter 6, if you choose the right lamp based on your space and needs and you choose the light bulb based on the role it will play (e.g., the level of light), you will be successful in meeting your lighting needs. How you design your learning environment and the accompanying goal determines how well your students can work within that learning environment. Specifying the goal clarifies the purpose of the lesson, providing you and your students with a starting point from which to work. While the goal tells them what they will be learning, their ability to access that learning experience depends heavily on the environment. It's about providing opportunities to learn; those opportunities are provided via the design.

Designing Goals

To accomplish the previously mentioned practices, you must determine a focus for your lesson. You need to identify the outcomes you want the students to achieve.

CHOOSING THE GOAL: MATT ROBERTS AND THE STUDENT PATH Matt Roberts believes that the goal directs not only the lesson's path but also the work that his middle school students do. To introduce the lesson each day he writes the lesson goal on the board, but sometimes there is information within the math text that provides additional introductory information. In both cases, he points out the goal to the students at the beginning of each lesson. The goal, as he sees it, gets the students thinking about what situations or problems they're going to be addressing that day. To him, the goal designates the path on which they are going to walk.

What is it that you want them to experience? Do you want to have summative or formative assessments within the lesson? Is this an introductory lesson, a culminating lesson, or something in between? The most important question, though, is what skills or content knowledge will they gain by being in your classroom on this particular day? To get started, many teachers turn to state standards.

The following example follows the suggestion to select first the standard from which you are going to work. Next, you determine what within that standard will be your focus for that day. Even though you will sometimes address multiple standards in one lesson, to minimize confusion this example pulls from just one standard. The following is a general description of a lesson using the CCSS Grade 4 Language Standard L.4.2.:

> Demonstrate command of the conventions of standard English capitalization, punctuation, and spelling when writing. Use correct capitalization. Use commas and quotation marks to mark direct speech and quotations from a text. Use a comma before a coordinating conjunction in a compound sentence. Spell grade-appropriate words correctly, consulting references as needed. (National Governors Association for Best Practices and the Council of Chief State School Officers, 2010)

Scenario Before now, the students have practiced the use of the capitalization, commas, quotation marks, and have worked on their related spelling words. The teacher has seen, though, that the students aren't demonstrating a full understanding of commas when using coordinating conjunctions. She wants to focus on this comma issue.

Other than the typical school supplies, each student has a small 11-in. x 8-in. whiteboard and dry-erase markers at their desk. They are accustomed to being out of their seats and presenting information to the class either as individuals or as a part of a group. The teacher tends to emphasize collaboration over competition by designing situations where students develop and create materials together. Understanding the need for balance, she also strategically designs situations where students demonstrate individual growth and leadership.

The Initial Goal Students will add commas appropriately to coordinating conjunctions during sentence writing practice.

At first this looks like a great goal. It specifies what the teacher wants the students to do. If you look a little more closely, however, this goal is limiting. The end of the goal references "sentence writing practice." Although this might feel specific and easily identifiable to the teacher, it could get in the way of attempting other activities during the lesson. To meet this goal, the students must show their understanding of coordinating conjunctions through the process of writing. That simple statement limits how the students demonstrate their knowledge to sentence writing practice. Although the suggestions from the National Governors Association Center for Best Practices and Council of Chief State School Officers (CCSS Grade 4 Language Standard L.4.2) mentioned alternatives, the following example of a UDL-friendly goal demonstrates how this piece of the writing process can be practiced to develop an understanding across the class, which could lead to an improved outcome in writing, whether through the use of a scribe, computer, or speech-to-text technology.

Universal Design for Learning-Friendly Goal Students will demonstrate the appropriate use of commas within coordinating conjunctions.

By writing this goal, the teacher opens the door to activities that support writing. For example, the teacher might write coordinating conjunctions onto card stock, which are distributed throughout the classroom to pairs of students. Pairs find other pairs with another coordinating conjunction to create a full sentence. To increase involvement even more, the teacher might have the correct number of commas on other placards, which are held by students, who stand in the "comma corral." They wait until the teams have identified their pairs, then they ask for a comma. Next, the teacher could ask the students to stand in a line, placing the important comma person in the right spot. The process allows students to gain an understanding of comma placement and coordinating conjunctions all while allowing for structured movement, collaboration, and decision making.

Although it is true that students will ultimately need to demonstrate their understanding of comma placement within coordinating conjunctions through sentence writing, giving them opportunities to connect with purpose and operation of the comma through physical activity, cooperative activities, and group practice and then following that up with knowledge transfer opportunities (examples in writing), the students are more likely to achieve the goal. The goal is for them to demonstrate their knowledge, and the teacher has created a lesson around that goal and a learning environment, which supports all students in their movement toward that goal.

Choosing the Right Words

In Chapter 2 I gave you a list of verbs that can be used to write open goals. Table 7.3, created by Kizlik (2012), provides additional words but with an explanation of those words.

Table 7.3. Verbs for open-ended goals

Words: Apply a rule

Definition: To state a rule as it applies to a situation, object or event that is being analyzed. The statement must convey analysis of a problem situation and/or its solution, together with the name or statement of the rule that was applied.

Word: Assess

Definition: To stipulate the conditions by which the behavior specified in an objective may be ascertained. Such stipulations are usually in the form of written descriptions. For obvious reasons, assess is rarely used as a verb in learning objectives at the elementary school level.

Word: Classify

Definition: To place objects, words, or situations into categories according to defined criteria for each category. The criteria must be made known to the student.

Word: Compose

Definition: To formulate a composition in written, spoken, musical or artistic form.

Word: Construct

Definition: To make a drawing, structure, or model that identifies a designated object or set of conditions.

(continued)

Table 7.3. (*continued*)

Word: Define

Definition: To stipulate the requirements for inclusion of an object, word, or situation in a category or class. Elements of one or both of the following must be included: (1) The characteristics of the words, objects, or situations that are included in the class or category. (2) The characteristics of the words, objects, or situations that are excluded in the class or category. To define is to set up criteria for classification.

Word: Demonstrate

Definition: The student performs the operations necessary for the application of an instrument, model, device, or implement. Note: There is a temptation to use *demonstrate* in objectives such as, "the student will demonstrate his knowledge of vowel sounds." As the verb is defined, this is improper use of it.

Word: Describe

Definition: To name all of the necessary categories of objects, object properties, or event properties that are relevant to the description of a designated situation. The objective is of the form. "The student will describe this order, object, or event," and does not limit the categories that may be used in mentioning them. Specific or categorical limitations, if any, are to be given in the performance standards of each objective. When using this verb in an objective, it is helpful to include a statement to the effect of what the description, as a minimum, must reference.

Word: Diagram

Definition: To construct a drawing with labels and with a specified organization or structure to demonstrate knowledge of that organization or structure. Graphic charting and mapping are types of diagramming, and these terms may be used where more exact communication of the structure of the situation and response is desired.

Word: Distinguish

Definition: To identify under conditions when only two contrasting identifications are involved for each response.

Word: Estimate

Definition: To assess the dimension of an object, series of objects, event or condition without applying a standard scale or measuring device. Logical techniques of estimation, such as are involved in mathematical interpolation, may be used. See Measure.

Word: Evaluate

Definition: To classify objects, situations, people, conditions, etc., according to defined criteria of quality. Indication of quality must be given in the defined criteria of each class category. Evaluation differs from general classification only in this respect.

Word: Identify

Definition: To indicate the selection of an object of a class in response to its class name, by pointing, picking up, underlining, marking, or other responses.

Word: Interpret

Definition: To translate information from observation, charts, tables, graphs, and written material in a verifiable manner.

Word: Label

Definition: To stipulate a verbal (oral or written) response to a given object, drawing, or composition that contains information relative to the known, but unspecified structure of these objects, drawings, or compositions. Labeling is a complex behavior that contains elements of naming and identifying.

Word: Locate

Definition: To stipulate the position of an object, place, or event in relation to other specified objects, places, or events. Ideational guides to location such as grids, order arrangements and time may be used to describe location. Note: Locate is not to be confused with Identify.

Word: Measure

Definition: To apply a standard scale or measuring device to an object, series of objects, events, or conditions, according to practices accepted by those who are skilled in the use of the device or scale.

Word: Name

Definition: To supply the correct name, in oral or written form for an object, class of objects, persons, places, conditions, or events which are pointed out or described.

Word: Order

Definition: To arrange two or more objects or events in accordance with stated criteria.

Word: Predict

Definition: To use a rule or principle to predict an outcome or to infer some consequence. It is not necessary that the rule or principle be stated.

Word: Reproduce

Definition: To imitate or copy an action, construction, or object that is presented.

Word: Solve

Definition: To effect a solution to a given problem, in writing or orally. The problem solution must contain all the elements required for the requested solution, and may contain extraneous elements that are not required for solution. The problem must be posed in such a way that the student is able to determine the type of response that is acceptable.

Words: State a rule

Definition: To make a statement that conveys the meaning of the rule, theory or principle.

Word: Translate

Definition: To transcribe one symbolic form to another of the same or similar meaning.

From Kizlik, R. (2012). *Definitions of behavioral verbs for learning opportunities.* Boca Raton, FL: Robert Kizlik & Associates; reprinted by permission. Retrieved from http://www.adprima.com/verbs.htm

Much of goal writing is about choosing the right words. We want the students to know what they are going to do before they begin the lesson. This triggers the affective network, opening an opportunity for the principle of Engagement to come to life.

Student Ownership

We write our lesson goal up on the board, and we quickly go over it at the beginning of the lesson. This is because we want our students to know what is coming.
—Julie Calfee, English teacher, high school

The ownership of learning by students is crucial to their educational experience. For those of us in the classroom, this can be a quandary at times. We ask, "How do I get them to take ownership when their fascination lies in something outside of the classroom?"

A key theme in research in student ownership boils down to relationships. A 1992 study by Phelan, Davidson, and Cao (p. 698) found that this sentiment from a student—"the way teachers treat you as a student—as a person, really"—was more important than any other indicator to the students' commitment to goals. Students want to be seen and recognized for the people they are. This vein of research continues to be studied and validated throughout the literature. To date, we know that elementary, middle, and high school students all want teachers to have a quality relationship with them and help them in their learning (Baker, Grant & Morlock, 2008; Janay, Sharkey, Olivarri, Tanigawa, & Mauseth, 2010; Pianta, Belsky, Vandergrift, Houts, & Morrison, 2008; Pianta & Stuhlman, 2004; Sander et al., 2010). The UDL framework provides opportunities for this kind of connection and it supports growth in student ownership. Let's return to the idea that the framework is a decision-making tool. Using it in that way can inform the choice process.

When you read the guidelines, you see multiple opportunities to connect with students as people. For example, one way you can "provide options for comprehension" (one of the guidelines) is to "activate or supply background knowledge." Even knowing the broad interest base of most of your students will help you connect the goal of the lesson to the interests of your students, but you must do that for them. Music icons, the latest book series, popular smart-phone or tablet applications, and student-preferred television shows can provide examples. And if you're not connected to any of these outlets, you can get that same information from your most informed source—the students. Use moments between classes, during passing periods, or when you're walking to the parking lot at the end of the day to find minimoments when you can find out this kind of information. These very moments affect the learning of your students.

Moving to the principle of Action and Expression, if you look at the guideline "provide options for executive functions," there are multiple opportunities to build interpersonal connections with your students. We'll focus in on the checkpoint "support planning and strategy development." If in the design of your learning environment you assist your students in keeping a calendar of assignments, you could remind them to study for a specific assessment activity as it relates to the goal of the lesson. If your students are unfamiliar with study skills, they will need help in breaking down their study steps. Offering them concrete ideas helps them take ownership of their studying. In addition, have side conversations with students you know need additional support (e.g., "Cyan, I know you do really well when you make study cards. If you make two new ones each day and study them, you will have all 10 terms memorized this week. You're also great with diagrams. Why don't you make a diagram of how these 10 terms fit together? Before you know it you will be ready for next week"). You might not be giving a written test the next week, but you will eventually assess Cyan's knowledge of those terms, and he will need to know and understand them. This kind of specific guidance helps Cyan become a decision maker in his own educational path. He now has some ideas with which to work, and with your encouragement he can move toward accomplishing the goal that has been given. Students' ownership of their learning is a strong indicator of a successful learner (Pianta et al., 2008). By clearly identifying the goal of the lesson and then posting that goal, you provide your students with another opportunity to take ownership.

SETTING THE GOALS: MATT ROBERTS AND THE STUDENT'S
PERSPECTIVE   Matt Roberts considers the students' point of view when
he designs his lesson goals. He begins this by asking student centered
questions (e.g., What is it that I'm going to be capable of doing that I
wasn't able to do prior to that? What skills will I have? What knowledge
base will I have?). He then melds those with the teacher perspective of
standards to create goals that encompass both. He clarifies that his goals
allow the students to experience flexibility in their delivery of information
or products.

THE LESSON PLAN

I now keep my UDL graphic organizer next to me, and I also think about my student population and ask, "What is something that sometimes gets in the way of
them learning?" Because everybody is going to come at it in a different way, I
need for my lessons to have lots of ways to learn.

—Patrice Goble, fifth-grade teacher

The process of lesson development is largely guided by individual choice and
preference.

How you approach lesson development is going to depend on several dynamics: personal preference, building-level or district-level requirements, text-based or
online formats. For this reason, it's difficult to suggest that one format is better than
another. What's more important is what you are asking yourself while developing
the lesson.

The Purpose Behind Lesson Planning

Lesson planning is at the heart of lesson delivery, but the process you use can either support or restrict your use of UDL. After some experience, lesson planning
can become a straightforward process. You organize what your students are going
to do, when they're going to do it, and how they're going to show you they learned
something. UDL doesn't complicate the process; instead, the aspects of lesson development are more tightly defined, opening doors of opportunity for you and your
students.

Analysis of Lesson Plan Development

After synthesizing over 800 studies that analyzed achievement in the classroom,
Hattie (2009, p. 239) came to an important conclusion about the complex nature of
lessons and what teachers must do to create successful lessons:

Teachers need to identify clearly what they want their students to learn,
Identify how they will measure their students' success,
Identify whether or not their class as a whole are achieving, and
Look at the gap between student achievement and their own planning and ask,
"Where are you going?" "How are you going?" and "Where to next?"

The focus on learning intentions and success criterion speak to the importance of a lesson's goal. As discussed earlier, both the intentions of your lesson and the desired outcome need to be in your goal. What is it that you want your students to walk away with at the end of the lesson?

Hattie's belief that successful lessons also focus on the students' attainment of information, their outcome data, and any gaps between the two all speak directly to the broad design of the lesson (i.e., the use of the UDL principles). His three questions, to be used simultaneously by students and teachers, are also in line with the UDL framework's desired outcomes of resourceful, knowledgeable, strategic, goal-directed, purposeful, and motivated students (Meyer, Rose, & Gordon, 2013). Hattie argued that to reach these outcomes, teaching and learning should be visible. His interpretation of visibility is accomplished through the teacher's specific and supportive feedback, an underlying checkpoint under the principle of Engagement. In addition, woven through his quote is the concept of lesson analysis. These aspects of lesson development can be further investigated by looking closely at what some authors have determined as key components within successful lesson planning.

Fenty, McDuffie-Landrum, and Fisher (2012) named five effective teaching practices. Pulling from work by Duke and Pearson (2002) and Fisher and Frey (2007), they concluded that each lesson needs to have

- An anticipatory set

- Modeling

- Guided practice

- Independent practice

- Closure

Anticipatory Set

Early automobiles with internal-combustion engines did not start automatically. A person had to place a crank into the crankshaft at the front of the car and turn it clockwise with considerable vigor. This process would cause the pistons to move, making the spark plugs ignite the fuel, which would start the engine. Similar to the early cars, a lesson needs a specific activity designed to fire the pistons and start the engines of our students' brains.

Whether called the anticipatory set (Hunter, 1994), the exploratory introduction (Sunal, McCormick, Sunal, & Shwery, 2005), exploratory phase (Flynn, Mesibov, Vermette, & Smith, 2004; Jones, Vermette, & Jones, 2009) or preparation for work (Brunn, 2010), this is where you quickly grab the attention of the student. The activity might be brief (Hunter, 1994) or it might take longer so as to establish a solid base from which to work (Jones et al., 2011). The activities can be designed to entice interest (e.g., provide options for recruiting interest under the principle of Engagement), establish relevance (mentioned within that same guideline), or work within the students' background knowledge (e.g., provide options for comprehension under the principle of Representation). To minimize confusion, I'll use the term *anticipatory set* for this section.

Always making sure the activity is congruent with the goal of the lesson; the idea is to move steadily through this part of the lesson so you can get into the meat of it. Critiqued by some for having the potential to be too superficial (Johnson, 2000; Jones et al., 2011), the concept behind the anticipatory set is very important within a UDL-designed lesson. This is where you determine how you will draw in and maintain your students' interest. It would be a mistake, though, to limit your thinking of the anticipatory set to the principle of Engagement or the one guideline under Representation mentioned previously. The design of the lesson is where you truly begin to see how the guidelines of UDL all interlace with one another to support your students' learning.

Let's return to the example of heat transfer in Chapter 3, which focused on bringing relevancy, value, and authenticity to the lesson through the use of hot beverages. Within that example were traces of Representation where the discussion was not just verbal. It included the creation of a "T" table on the board, and the physics teacher also tapped into the students' background knowledge, hoping to establish a platform for the transfer and generalization of their knowledge. These were seamlessly woven into that anticipatory activity, helping ensure a greater level of connection to the lesson.

Modeling

This literally named practice encourages the teacher to take the students through the steps within a strategy, the order of operations within an algorithm, or the stages of a development. This is meant to be a time when teachers observe whether students have a firm understanding before they move into guided or independent practice. However, what if you find modeling to be too teacher-centered and you want to move into more inquiry-based practices?

By focusing on lesson planning and questioning techniques, Black (2005) stated that teachers can use modeling to establish the problem or concept for the students. Although his work focuses on science education, these suggestions can be applied to lessons across disciplines:

- You need to know the breakdown of the concepts within your lesson plan and how they directly link to your goal, but do not state them to your students.

- Ask your students open-ended questions during the demonstration (Why do you think …?)

- Elicit from your students' predictions and hypotheses. Have the students suggest potential conclusions. (What do you think will happen if …?)

- Include students during the demonstration. Invite them to be a part of the procedure by assisting with material setup.

- Support active observation. You can do this by providing them with structures for diagramming, illustration, and so forth. Journaling is another strategy for active observation.

Guided Practice versus Independent Practice

Guided practice comes before independent practice and is structured with supports from peers and teachers (Fenty et al., 2012). Supports refer to any structures or person-to-person interactions that help the students move toward an initial and then deeper understanding of the skill or concept. Independent practice should be designed to strengthen the skills acquired by the students. While they work independently, they apply the newly learned skill or concept to a new situation. This demonstrates their ability to transfer and generalize the information, which means they are more likely to be able to do the same in the future (Fenty et al., 2012). In both cases, the built-in structures can encompass multiple guidelines and often include scaffolding.

Both guided and individual practice can be interlaced with options listed under the principle of Representation. For example, if your students are working with symbols, you might bring in graphics or text to support their understanding, or the lesson's original design might have been limited to a visual design but you can broaden the opportunities provided to your students by adding an auditory component. A quick scan through Chapter 4 will remind you of the myriad options.

Focusing on the principle of Action and Expression, both guided and individual practices should have formative assessment underlying them. A snag experienced by student teachers and early career teachers, as identified by Jones et al. (2011), was the propensity of this group to either use homework as a way to combine practice and grades, discussion as the sole way to gather evidence of understanding, or the use of rote-memorization tests or multiple-choice tests.

The first is wrought with issues around fidelity (e.g., did the student complete the homework independently) and creates a confluence between two independent factors—the rate of completion (i.e., how many problems the student completed) versus the level of understanding (i.e., whether the student answered the problems correctly). Going back to the discussion on assessment in Chapter 5, any assessment should 1) directly link back to the lesson goal and 2) provide clear data on the students' understanding of a concept or skill. When you mix in the rate completion, you have now muddled those data you were hoping to use to understand your students' level of understanding.

The second example is another misunderstood method of gathering information. It's natural to think that through a conversation, you're going to gather information about a students' understanding of a concept or skill. Jones et al. (2012) encourage teachers to add in a tangible product as a demonstration of understanding. Furthermore, they assert that this tangible product be along the lines of an authentic assessment (Wiggins, 1990).

An authentic assessment is one that brings relevance and authenticity into assessments. They tend to be scenario based and require problem solving by the students rather than having them respond to questions with definitive answers (Darling-Hammond, 1997). Pulled from work by Dana and Tippens (1993), Moon,

Brighton, Callahan, and Robinson (2005, p. 120) summarized the characteristics of authentic assessment as

1. focused on content that is essential, focusing on the big ideas or concepts, rather than trivial microfacts or specialized skills;

2. in-depth in that they lead to other problems and questions;

3. feasible and can be done easily and safely within a school and classroom;

4. focused on the ability to produce a quality product or performance, rather than a single right answer;

5. promoting the development and display of student strengths and expertise (the focus is on what the student knows);

6. having criteria that are known, understood, and negotiated between the teacher and student before the assessment begins;

7. providing multiple ways in which students can demonstrate they have met the criteria, allowing multiple points of view and multiple interpretations;

8. requiring scoring that focuses on the essence of the task and not what is easiest to score.

Closure

Within the lesson format, this is the time set aside to assess the students' level of understanding. It is an extremely important step because it gives you one more opportunity to check in on the students' levels of understanding. Exit slips, discussed earlier in this chapter, are just one tool to use for this stage. Another format is called 3-2-1. You determine what topics will be shared associated with those amounts. For example, if the lesson goal reads, "Students will demonstrate their knowledge of soccer rules, player positions, and safety concerns." For the concluding 3-2-1 activity, you have the students volunteer to name three positions played on the soccer field, two actions that would earn a player a penalty, and one piece of safety equipment that must be worn on the field.

Table 7.4 includes additional closure activities. This list should not be considered complete. Instead, allow these suggested activities to inspire new ideas that you can use in your own classroom.

One additional note about closure activities—make sure that your use of a closure activity aligns with the UDL framework. Through your use of the framework, you will know exactly *why* you are using the activity and what potential barriers need to be addressed (e.g., do all students have the equal ability to respond during a full class discussion?). Equally as important, these are only useful activities if they are structured to tie directly back to the stated goal.

The anticipation set, modeling, guided practice, independent practice, and closure lay out the important components of lesson design, but the act of teaching can be complicated by other design issues. Briefly mentioned earlier in this chapter, Jones et al. (2011) identified six pitfalls they have seen preservice and early service teachers experience. Table 7.5 lists those issues and summarizes the authors'

Table 7.4.   Closure activities

Activity: Postcards

Tools: Notecards

Process: Have students write a postcard to a person who is not in the classroom about an identified skill, concept, or topic they learned

Reason: Allows students to reflect on what they learned

Activity: 3-2-1

Tools: Sheet of paper

Process: Students write about 3 things discussed, 2 things they learned, and 1 thing they are still unclear about

Reason: Allows students to reflect on what they learned

Activity: Muddy water

Tools: Sheet of paper

Process: Write down 1 thing you understand and 1 thing that is unclear

Reason: Allows students to reflect on what they learned

Activity: Anticipation guide wrap-up

Tools: Use previous anticipation guide

Process: Students correct any previous misconceptions they had with the introductory anticipation guide

Reason: Students are able to fix their mistakes

Activity: Beach ball

Tools: Beach ball with questions

Process: Students pass around beach ball and whichever question their hand falls on, that's the question they must answer

Reason: Get the students to think about what they know and do not know

Activity: Don't say "ugh"

Tools: Ball

Process: Students pass around a ball and must repeat the last thing the person before them said and say something about the topic that has not been said

Reason: Get the students to think about what they know and do not know

Activity: Closure log

Tools: Notebooks/spirals

Process: Students keep a notebook summarizing the day's activity

Reason: Allows students to reflect on what they learned

Activity: Dimes and pennies

Tools: Paper

Process: Students rate the day's class and list one way to improve the experience

Reason: Get the students to think about what they know and do not know

Activity: Ticket out the door

Tools: Paper

Process: Students write down one thing they understand

Reason: Allows students to reflect on what they learned

Activity: Fill in the blank

Tools: Paper

Process: Teacher writes a statement and leaves the keyword out; students must write the statement and include the missing word

Reason: Allows students to reflect on what they learned

Activity: Before and after

Tools: Paper

Process: Students must write the process/step that occurred before and after the selected step

Reason: Allows students to reflect on what they learned

Activity: Checklist form

Tools: None

Process: Students will receive a completeness/quality checklist during the last five minutes of class. Students will complete the checklist stating what they completed and any questions they may have. The teacher will use the checklist to provide the student feedback

Reason: Allows students to reflect on what they learned

Activity: Questions from the day's lesson

Tools: None

Process: The teachers will ask questions from the day's lesson. Students will turn their thumbs up or down depending on whether the answer is yes (up) or no (down)

Reason: Allows students to reflect on what they learned

Activity: Ticket under the seat

Tools: Paper, scissors and tape.

Process: Take questions/concepts and randomly place them under desks. The person or group that gets a question has to give the answer or explain the concept

Reason: Allows students to reflect on what they learned

Activity: Smiley says . . .

Tools: Students can write on their own paper or teacher can have premade Smiley sheets.

Process: Students must respond to the prompts: *J I really understood . . . K I have a few questions about before I can say I fully understand. L I do not understand* at all

Reason: Get the students to think about what they know and do not know

Activity: I care WHY (or WHY do I care)?

Tools: Paper if teacher wants this to be a Quick Write activity, but it can be done orally.

Process: Students must explain the relevancy of the concepts learned to their lives and how they might use them

Reason: Creates relevancy with students so that they see life connections

Activity: We're going where?

Tools: Paper, writing utensil or interactive white board writing caption tool.

Process: Students predict the topic of the next class lesson. Write it on paper or on the interactive white board. Refer to the prediction (as interactive white board captured image if possible) as an opener for the next class session or during closure

Reason: Can be used as review

Activity: Who's got it next?

Tools: Small ball or stuffed animals to toss

Process: Teacher starts by tossing the item to a student and asking them to tell one thing they learned. That student tosses to another student who must also tell what they have learned from the day's lesson. Teacher can also say a specific vocabulary term or concept only, toss and have the students do the same

(continued)

Table 7.4. (*continued*)

Reason: Allows students to reflect on what they learned

Activity: Freestyle

Tools: No materials needed

Process: Teacher writes/states the main idea of the day's lesson. In groups, students have 2–5 minutes to discuss concepts surrounding that main idea. One person from the group, someone who likes to garner attention, must freestyle (rap) a summary (1–3 minutes). Works best with boys. Can be taped and used as part of review

Reason: Allows students to reflect on what they learned. Showcases student creativity

Activity: It looks like this

Tools: Objects or images that relate to the lesson

Process: Teacher displays an object (or shows an image on the Interactive WhiteBoard) that directly relates to the day's lesson. Students must explain how the object/image connects to the day's concept

Reason: Allows students to reflect on what they learned

Activity: Take a stand!

Tools: Questions, PowerPoint

Process: Teacher asks questions that can be answered with TRUE or FALSE. If the answer is TRUE, students will stand. If FALSE, they will remain seated.

Reason: Allows students to reflect on what they learned

Activity: Doodling

Tools: Paper and writing utensils

Process: Students create pictures of what they learned that day

Reason: Allows students to reflect on what they learned

Source: Adapted from Booker T. Washington High School. (n.d.). *Closure spaces*. Retrieved from http://btwteachers. wikispaces.com/Closure+Activities

suggested solutions. If you're a seasoned teacher, you will likely nod your head; remembering your own experience with these situations or these examples might provide you with reflection points.

A Lesson Plan Format

This section reviewed the common components of the lesson plan and closed giving some examples of identified missteps that can occur when moving from planning to the act of teaching. If you are not comfortable with the lesson planning format you are using or you are looking for one that directly speaks to UDL, I suggest you create an account with CAST's UDL Exchange (http://udlexchange.cast.org/home).

UDL Exchange is a robust site where participants can create, store, share, and search for resources, lessons, and units. Because the site supports teachers worldwide, it uses broader terms to define some of the things we've talked about in this book. I suggest you watch the video on the homepage before you create an account log-in and password. That way, once you're in the site, you'll feel a bit more comfortable negotiating it. You can always go back to the video. I also suggest you click on the far right tab at the top of the page titled "Feature Guide." This guide is a linear layout of the site and includes graphics to help you become acquainted with the site.

Table 7.5. The pitfalls

The mistake: An unclear learning objective (the goal)

The solution: Narrow the lesson goal to guide the specific content of the lesson. The goal should identify what piece of knowledge, skill, or competency the students will hold when they leave the classroom that day.

The mistake: Unfocused assessments or homework used as assessment

The solution: Have students create tangible products that demonstrate their new, modified, or complete knowledge of the subject, skill, or competency. These products must be constructed to reflect the specified learning goal. In addition, homework should be designed for skill-building and not counted as assessment (i.e., graded for accuracy).

The mistake: Students emerging ideas are not tracked

The solution: Use activities to provide summative data rather than formal assessments or primarily depending upon discussion.

The mistake: The purpose of the assessment doesn't match the lesson's goal

The solution: Directly link the goal statement to the design of any assessments. One strategy is to design those two pieces together, then build the lesson.

The mistake: Unclear on how to start the lesson

The solution: Plan a meaningful introduction with a focus on depth and not brevity of time. Consider this part of the lesson as the base on which your students will stand for the remainder of the lesson.

The mistake: Students are vessels into which information is poured

The solution: Focus on providing students the opportunity to synthesize information or apply their new knowledge to unique situations. Closely examine the amount of time the lesson is teacher-focused. Begin to add in planned time where the activities are student-led.

Source: Jones, Jones, and Vermette (2011).

Once you're logged in, you will see a box titled "Getting Started: Three Types of Materials." You can choose UDL Resources, UDL Lessons, or UDL Collections. Resources are any type of digitally based materials you would use for a lesson. These can include self-made documents, articles, pictures, or videos. Any of these files can be up to 2 megabytes in size. Lessons are just that, lessons. I will talk more about the design of those in the following section of this chapter. The collections can be thought of as teaching units.

A collection is a compilation of any resources and/or lessons you wish to bring together. For example, you might be teaching a lesson on the Salem witch trials and already have a lesson plan. However, you locate resources through UDL Exchange and upload several others and want to keep them organized. You can do this by creating a collection. As you browse through UDL Exchange, you will find hundreds of examples and suggestions from teachers and teacher leaders. At this point, I am going to return to the lesson development piece of that web site.

If you click on the center tab at the top of your screen titled, "Build," you will then go to a screen that gives you the option of creating a new lesson, resource, or collection. Click on "lesson." Although I am not going to give you a tutorial on how to use this online resource (you can use the supports I mentioned previously or you can click on any of the Lesson Supports at the top of the page), I am going to highlight certain pieces of this tool.

You will see that this design structure was developed to help you think through things such as the background knowledge your students need to have to be successful during the lesson, the purpose behind the lesson, and its connection to the CCSS (which are uploaded to this site and can be selected based on the subject area). There is a location to list your instructional goal, subsequent objectives, and a place to put down your thoughts on how your lesson will address the needs of the variable learners present. Underneath that you lay out your opening method, what you will do during the lesson, and your closing activities. At the bottom, this tool provides a space for you to list the materials and resources you're going to use for the lesson. Next to each header you'll see a lower case letter within a small circle. These open boxes with written descriptions to support your understanding of that header. These same supports provide the definitions of terms that might be unfamiliar to you.

I stress again that this is just one lesson design tool that you can use. This tool does not have an internal checklist or monitoring system that investigates your use of UDL. In fact, it doesn't even mention the three principles. So, how does it connect to UDL? The benefit to this tool is that it uses the vocabulary of UDL, was designed using the framework so you have the supports you need to understand the tool, and is housed within a web site that has other resources and information designed with UDL in mind. It is also a layout that is familiar to teachers if you are working to become familiar with the framework, I suggest you have it (or this book) next to you as you begin using this tool.

A CHECKLIST

There are no firm steps that will tell you that you are using UDL to its fullest or that you are planning a UDL lesson. In an effort to investigate the effect of UDL knowledge on lesson design, some have investigated the number of modifications or options teachers offered as well as clear instruction within their lessons to indicate their use of the framework (Spooner, Baker, Harris, Ahlgrim-Delzell, & Browder, 2007) while others used a lesson plan format investigating preservice teachers' procedures, materials used, barriers addressed, and the use of the UDL principles (Williams, Evans, & King, 2012). In both cases, the researchers found that teachers needed direct instruction on UDL to affect their ability to design lessons that could lead to more accessible learning environments and lessons.

The three sections of this book were designed to give you the information you need to not only design a lesson based on the UDL framework but also create a learning environment that supports the delivery of that lesson. Even though there is no definitive lesson plan format or checklist you can hand to another teacher, administrator, or other stakeholder that says you are effectively using UDL, there are some reflective questions you can ask yourself that will help you decide if you're headed in a direction in harmony with UDL.

When I plan my lessons, do I

– Have a clear goal? (see the section on Goals at the beginning of this chapter)

– Know how I'm going to measure whether students have met that goal? (see the sections on Guided and Independent Practice and Closure)

– Create activities and assignments that guide students toward the lesson goal? (see The Role of Goals)

– Create activities and assignments designed with options mentioned under the three principles of Engagement, Representation, and Action and Expression? (see Chapters 3, 4, & 5)

– Create assessments directly related to the lesson's goal? (see Chapter 6 and Examining Achievement)

– Create assessments designed with the options listed under Action and Expression? (see Chapter 5)

– Use a variety of tools and resources to create my lesson plans? (see Chapter 6)

CONCLUSION

This chapter introduced two key elements of UDL designed learning—the goal and the lesson. The role of the goal is to provide a direction for the lesson. This direction is crucial to the success of your lesson. The chapter referenced the use of the CCSS during lesson development and offered suggestions on how to frame your goals to meet the standards but create a UDL-friendly environment. The section ended with the important topic of student ownership. Students are attentive to the types of interactions they have with their teachers and the learning environment. When those interactions are positive (e.g., teachers are friendly, approachable, kind, use humor) and the environment is varied (e.g., variety of examples, approaches), students report that they are more connected with their learning outcomes (Patrick & Ryan, 2009). For students to be successful in the pre-K–12 environment and beyond, we must support their growth in their ownership of their learning. The research connecting cognition and emotion is growing rapidly, providing hard evidence that the emotional experiences our students have in relation to learning are strong, influential, and long lasting (Immordino-Yang & Damasio, 2007; Rappolt-Schlichtmann, Daley & Rose, 2012; Storbeck & Clore, 2012). As teachers, we can create an accessible pathway by using the framework of UDL.

The remainder of the chapter focused on the development of the lesson plan. Using the five overarching areas of anticipatory set, modeling, guided practice, independent practice, and conclusion, the section discussed the necessity of these elements within a lesson designed using the UDL principles. Next, six pitfalls identified through research were presented as an introduction for newer teachers and a reminder to those who are seasoned. A lesson plan tool designed by researchers at CAST was presented and described with tips on how to use the tool. Finally, a self-reflection checklist for teachers to use during lesson design was offered. Although I attempted to provide a wide range of scenarios throughout this book to demonstrate what the application of lessons might look like, it is no simple feat to move from a lesson plan to the execution of that plan. The dynamics of space, intrapersonal relationships with students and other adults, and the responsibilities teachers hold outside of instruction turn what some might see as a linear process into one with myriad choices, situations, and outcomes. That said, when you have a powerful framework such as UDL, which allows for shifts and adjustments to ensure barriers to instruction are lessened, you can confidently design your learning environment and lessons and track the outcomes of your students.

Start small. Choose one focus within the framework. Choose one focus within your practice. Enlist the involvement of other teachers, and talk with each other about your experiences. Trade suggestions. Share successes. Watch for change.

"I keep piecing together each lesson and just adding more stuff based on UDL. Sometimes I think I'm adding too much and we're not getting anywhere, but that's because I was comfortable doing the same stuff all of the time. Now I'm getting good results in data. I'm seeing improvement in my students' results. I'm using UDL, and I know I am getting somewhere."

—Kathy Denniston, fifth-grade teacher

REFERENCES

Andrade, H., Huff, K., & Brooke, G. (2012). *Students at the center: Teaching and learning in the era of the Common Core*. Boston, MA: Jobs for the Future.

Apple Inc. (n.d.). *Accessibility*. Retrieved from http://www.apple.com/accessibility/

Baker, J.A., Grant, S., & Morlock, L. (2008). The teacher–student relationship as a developmental context for children with internalizing or externalizing behavior problems. *School Psychology Quarterly, 23*(1), 3–15.

Baloche, L.A. (1998). *The cooperative classroom: Empowering learning*. Upper Saddle River, NJ: Prentice Hall.

Bandura, A. (1986). *Social foundations of thought and action: A social cognitive theory*. Englewood Cliffs, NJ: Prentice Hall.

Bandura, A. (1993). Perceived self-efficacy in cognitive development and functioning. *Educational Psychologist, 28*(2), 117–148.

Bandura, A. (1997). *Self-efficacy: The exercise of control*. New York, NY: Freeman.

Beyer, C.J., & Davis, E.A. (2011). Learning to critique and adapt science curriculum materials: Examining the development of preservice teachers' pedagogical content knowledge. *Science Education, 96*(1), 130–157. doi:10.1002/sce.20466

Black, R. (2005). Why demonstrations matter: Teacher-centered demonstration still has a place in the constructivist classroom. *Science and Children, 43*(1), 52–55.

Black, S. (2002). Keeping kids in school. *American School Board Journal, 189*(12), 50–52.

Black, P., & Wiliam, D. (1998). Assessment and classroom learning. *Assessment in Education, 5*(1), 7–74. doi:10.1080/0969595980050102

Bodrova, E., Leong, D.J., & Akhutina, T.V. (2011). When everything new is well-forgotten old: Vygotsky/Luria insights in the development of executive functions. In R.M. Lerner, J.V. Lerner, E.P. Bowers, S. Lewin-Bizan, S. Gestsdottir, & J.B. Urban (Eds.), *Thriving in childhood and adolescence: The role of self-regulation processes: New Directions for Child and Adolescent Development, 133,* 11–28.

Booker T. Washington High School. (n.d.). *Closure spaces*. Licensed under a Creative Commons Attribution-ShareAlike 3.0 Unported License (http://creativecommons.org/licenses/by-sa/3.0/). Retrieved from http://btwteachers.wikispaces.com/Closure+Activities

Boyle, J.R. (2011). Thinking strategically to record notes in content classes. *American Secondary Education, 40*(1), 50–66.

Brookhart, S.M. (2007). Expanding views about formative assessment: A review of the literature. In H. McMillan (Ed.), *Formative assessment classroom: Theory into practice* (pp. 43–62). New York, NY: Teachers College Press.

Brookhart, S.M. (2012). Preventing feedback fizzle. *Educational Leadership,* 25–29.

Brown, M.W. (2009). The teacher–tool relationship: Theorizing the design and use of curriculum materials. In J.T. Remillard, B.A. Herbel-Eisenmann, & G.M. Lloyd (Eds.), *Mathematics teachers at work: Connecting curriculum materials and classroom instruction* (pp. 17–36). New York, NY: Routledge.

Brunn, NY, P. (2010). *The lesson planning handbook: Essential strategies that inspire student thinking and learning*. New York, NY: Scholastic.

Calkins, L., Ehrenworth, M., & Lehman, C. (2012). *Pathways to the Common Core: Accelerating achievement*. Portsmouth, NH: Heinemann.

CAST. (2011). *Types of evidence supporting UDL.* Wakefield, MA: Author. Retrieved from http://www.udlcenter.org/aboutudl/udlevidence

CAST. (2012a). *What is the national instructional materials accessibility standard (NIMAS)?* Wakefield, MA: Author. Retrieved http://aim.cast.org/learn/policy/federal/what_is_nimas

CAST. (2012b, August 12). *Acknowledging learner variability: Changes in UDL Guidelines 2.0.* Retrieved from http://www.udlcenter.org/resource_library/videos

CAST. (2012c). *What is the national instructional materials accessibility standard (NIMAS)?* Wakefield, MA: Author. Retrieved http://aim.cast.org/learn/policy/federal/what_is_nimas

Center for Mental Health in Schools at UCLA. (2006). *A technical aid packet on resource mapping and management to address barriers to learning: An intervention for systemic change.* Los Angeles, CA: Author.

Chappuis, S., & Stiggins, R.J. (2002). Classroom assessment for learning. *Educational Leadership, 60*(1), 40–43.

Cinnamond, J., & Zimpher, N. (1990). Reflectivity as a function of community. In R. Clift, W. Houston, & M. Pugach (Eds.), *Encouraging reflective practice in education: An analysis of issues and programmes* (pp. 57–72). New York, NY: Teachers College Press.

Clark, I. (2010). Formative assessment: "There is nothing so practical as good theory." *The Australian Journal of Education, 54*(3), 341–352.

Cohen, D.K., & Ball, D.L. (1999). *Instruction, capacity, and improvement* (CPRE Research Series RR-043). Philadelphia, PA: University of Pennsylvania Consortium for Policy Research in Education.

Cohen, E. (1994). Restructuring the classroom: Conditions for productive small groups. *Review of Educational Research, 64*(1), 1–35.

Colvin, G., Sugai, G., & Kameenui, E. (1994). *Curriculum for establishing a proactive school-wide discipline plan: Project Prepare.* Eugene, OR: University of Oregon, College of Education, Behavioral Research and Teaching.

Common Core State Standard Initiative. (2012). *About the standards.* Retrieved from www.corestandards.org/about-the-standards

Cooper, J.E., Horn, S., & Strahan, D.B. (2005). "If only they would do their homework": Promoting self-regulation in high school English classes. *High School Journal, 88*(3), 10–25.

Coyne, P., Ganley, P., Hall, T., Meo, G., Murray, E., & Gordon, D. (2009). Applying universal design for learning in the classroom. In D. Rose & A. Meyer (Eds.), *A practical reader in universal design for learning* (pp. 1–14). Cambridge, MA: Harvard University Press.

Coyne, P., Pisha, B., Dalton, B., Zeph, L.A., & Smith, N.C. (2012). Literacy by design: A universal design for learning approach for students with significant intellectual disabilities. *Remedial and Special Education, 33*(3), 162–172.

Craighead, E., & Ramanathan, H. (2007). Effective teacher interactions with English language learners in mainstream classes. *Mid-South Educational Research Association, 14*(1), 60–71.

Curtin, E. (2005). Instructional styles used by regular classroom teachers while teaching recently mainstreamed ESL students: Six urban middle school teachers in Texas share their experiences and perceptions. *Multicultural Education,* 36–42.

Dana, T.M., & Tippins, D.J. (1993). Considering alternative assessments for middle level learners. *Middle School Journal, 25*(2), 3–5.

Darling-Hammond, L. (1997). *The right to learn.* San Francisco, CA: Jossey-Bass.

Deci, E., & Ryan, R. (Eds.). (2002). *Handbook of self-determination research.* Rochester, NY: University of Rochester Press.

Dotterer, A.M., & Lowe, K. (2011). Classroom context, school engagement, and academic achievement and early adolescence. *Journal of Youth Adolescence, 40,* 1649–1660. doi:10.1007/210964–011–9647–5

DuFour, R., DuFour, R., & Eaker, R. (n.d.). *A big picture look at professional learning communities.* Retrieved from http://www.allthingsplc.info/pdf/links/brochure.pdf

Duke, N.K., & Pearson, D. (2002). Effective practices for developing reading comprehension. In A.E. Farstrup & S.J. Samuels (Eds.), *What research has to say about reading instruction* (3rd ed., pp. 205–242). Newark, DE: International Reading Association. doi:10.1598%2F0872071774.10

Eagleton, M.B., Guinee, K., & Langlais, K. (2009). Teaching internet literacy strategies: The hero inquiry project. In D.H. Rose & A. Meyer (Eds.), *A practical reader in universal design for learning* (pp. 149–162). Cambridge, MA: Harvard Education Press.

Easterbrooks, S.R., & Stephenson, B. (2006). An examination of twenty literacy, science, and methematics practices used to educate students who are deaf or hard of hearing. *American Annals of the Deaf, 151*(4), 385–395.

Edyburn, D. (2009). RTI and UDL interventions. *Journal of Special Education Technology, 24*(2), 46–47.

Edyburn, D. (2011). Harnessing the potential of technology to support the academic success of diverse students. *New Directions for Higher Education, 154,* 37–44.

Feedback loop. (2009). In *The American Heritage Dictionary of the English Language* (4th ed.). Retrieved from http://www.thefreedictionary.com/feedback+loop

Fenty, N.S., McDuffie-Landrum, K., & Fisher, G. (2012). Using collaboration, co-teaching, and question answer relationships to enhance content level literacy. *Teaching Exceptional Children, 44*(6), 28–37.

Fisher, D., & Frey, N. (2007). A tale of two middle schools: The difference in structure and instruction. *Journal of Adolescent and Adult Literacy, 51,* 204–221. doi:10.1598%2FJAAL.51.3.1

Fletcher-Carter, R., & Paez, D. (2010). Exploring the personal cultures of rural deaf/hard of hearing students. *Rural Special Education Quarterly, 29*(2), 18–24

Flynn, P., Mesibov, D., Vermette, P.J., & Smith, R.M. (2004). *Applying standards-based constructivism: A two-step guide for motivating middle and high school students.* Larchmont, NY: Eye on Education.

Fredrickson, B.L., & Branigan, C. (2005). Positive emotions broaden the scope of attention and thought–action repertoires. *Cognition and Emotion, 19*(3), 313–332.

Fuchs, D., Fuchs, L., & Burish, P. (2000). Peer-assisted learning strategies: An evidence-based practice to promote reading achievement. *Learning Disabilities Research & Practice, 15*(2), 85–91.

Furner, J., Yahya, N., & Duffy, M.L. (2005). Teach mathematics: Strategies to reach all students. *Intervention in School and Clinic, 41*(1), 16–23.

Furth, H.G. (1990). Creation of values. *American Psychologist, 45*(9), 1083–1084.

Gay, G. (2000). *Culturally responsive teaching: Theory, research & practice.* New York, NY: Teachers College Press.

Giangreco. M.F. (2007). *Absurdities and realities of special education: The complete digital set [CD].* Thousand Oaks, CA: Corwin Press.

Hall, T.E., Meyer, A., & Rose, D.H. (2012). An introduction to universal design for learning: Questions and answers. In T.E. Hall, A. Meyer, & D.H. Rose (Eds.), *Universal design for learning in the classroom: Practical applications* (pp. 1–8). New York, NY: The Guilford Press.

Hamre, B.K., & Pianta, R.C. (2001). Early teacher–child relationships and the trajectory of children's school outcomes through eighth grade. *Child Development, 72,* 625–638.

Hargreaves, A. (2007). Sustainable professional learning communities. In L. Stoll & K. Seashore Louis (Eds.), *Professional learning communities: Divergence, depth and dilemmas* (pp. 181–195). Maidenhead, England: Open University Press.

Harlen, W., & James, M. (1997). Assessment and learning: Differences and relationships between formative and summative assessments. *Assessment in Education, 4*(3), 365–379.

Harris, D., & MacRow-Hill, S.L. (1999). Application of Chroma-Gen haloscopic lenses to patients with dyslexia: A double-masked placebo-controlled trial. *Journal of the Optometric Association, 70*(1), 629–640.

Hattie, J. (2009). *Visible learning: A synthesis of over 800 meta-analyses relating to achievement.* New York, NY: Routledge.

Haydon, T., Maheady, L., & Hunter, W. (2010). Effects of numbers heads together on the daily quiz scores and on-task behavior of students with disabilities. *Journal of Behavior Education, 19,* 222–238. doi:10.1007/s10864–010–9108–3

Hiebert, J., Morris, A.K., Berk, D., & Jansen, D. (2007). Preparing teachers to learn from teaching. *Journal of Teacher Education, 58*(1), 47–61. doi: 10.1177/0022487106295726

Hipsher, C. (2009). 2009 U.S. Innovation Teachers Network: Columbus East High

School, Columbus, IN [Video file]. Retrieved from http://vimeo.com/6104437

Hunter, M. (1994). *Enhancing teaching.* New York, NY: MacMillan College.

Immordino-Yang., M. & Damasio, A. (2007). We feel, therefore we learn: The relevance of affective and social neuroscience to education. *Mind, Brain, and Education,* 1(1), 3-10.

Janay, J.B., Sharkey, J.D., Olivarri, R., Tanigawa, D.A., & Mauseth, T. (2010). A qualitative study of juvenile offenders, student engagement, and interpersonal relationships: Implications for research directions and preventionist approaches. *Journal of Educational and Psychological Consultants, 20,* 288–315. doi:10.1080/10474412.2010.522878

Jang, H., Reeve, J., & Deci, E. (2010). Engaging students in learning activities: It is not autonomy support of structure but autonomy support and structure. *Journal of Educational Psychology, 102*(3), 588–600.

Johnson, A.P. (2000). It's time for Madeline Hunter to go: A new look at lesson plan design. *Action in Teacher Education, 22*(1), 72–78. doi: 10.1080/01626620.2000.10462994

Johnson, D.W., & Johnson, R.T. (1999). Making cooperative learning work. *Theory Into Practice, 38,* 67–73.

Johnson, D.W., Johnson, R.T., & Holubec, E. (1991). *Cooperation in the classroom.* Edina, MN: Interaction Book Company.

Jones, J.L., & Dotson, K.B. (2010). Building the disposition of reflection through the inquiry-focused school library program. *School Libraries Worldwide, 16*(1), 33–46.

Jones, K.A., Jones, J., & Vermette, P.J. (2011). Six common lesson planning pitfalls: Recommendations for novice educators. *Education, 131*(4), 845–864.

Jones, K.A., Vermette, P.J., & Jones, J.L. (2009). An integration of "backwards planning" unit design with the "two-step" lesson planning framework. *Education, 130*(3), 357–360.

Kizlik, R. (2012). *Definitions of behavioral verbs for learning objectives.* Retrieved from http://www.adprima.com/verbs.htm

Koskinen, P., & Blum, I. (1986). Paired repeated reading: A classroom strategy for developing fluent reading. *The Reading Teacher, 40*(1), 70–75.

Lapinski, S., Gravel, J.A., & Rose, D.H. (2012). Tools for practice: The universal design for learning guidelines. In T.E. Hall, A. Meyer, & D.H. Rose (Eds.), *Universal design for learning in the classroom: Practical applications* (pp. 1–8). New York, NY: The Guilford Press.

Leahy, S., Lyon, C., Thompson, M. & Wiliam, D. (2005) Classroom assessment: Minute by minute, day by day. *Educational Leadership, 63*(3), 19-24.

Lewis, T.J., & Sugai, G. (1999). Effective behavior support: A systems approach to proactive school-wide management. *Focus on Exceptional Children, 31*(6), 1–24.

Lewis, T.J., Sugai, G., & Colvin, G. (1998). Reducing problem behavior through a school-wide system of effective behavioral support: Investigation of a school-wide social skills training program and contextual interventions. *School Psychology Review, 27,* 446–459.

Meyer, A., Rose, D.H., & Gordon, D.T. (2013). *Universal design for learning theory and practice.* Wakefield, MA: National Center on Universal Design for Learning.

Microsoft. (n.d.). *Microsoft accessibility.* Retrieved from http://www.microsoft.com/enable/

Miyake, A., Friedman, N.P., Emerson, M.J., Witzki, A.H., & Howerter, A. (2000). The unity and diversity of executive functions and their contributions to complex "frontallobe" tasks: A latent variable analysis. *Cognitive Psychology, 41,* 49–100.

Moon, T.R., Brighton, C.M., Callahan, C.M., & Robinson, A. (2005). Development of authentic assessments for the middle school classroom. *The Journal of Secondary Gifted Education, 16*(2/3), 119–133.

Morris, A.K., Hiebert, J., & Spitzer, S.M. (2009). Mathematical knowledge for teaching in planning and evaluating instruction: What can preservice teachers learn? *Journal for Research in Mathematics Education, 40*(5), 491–529.

National Governors Association Center for Best Practices and Council of Chief State School Officers. (2010). *Common Core State Standards for English language arts and literacy in history/social studies, science, and technical subjects.* Washington, DC: Author.

Nelson, T.H., Slavit, D., & Deuel, A. (2012). Two dimensions of an inquiry stance toward student-learning data. *Teachers College Record, 114,* 1–42.

Nieto, S. (2004). *Affirming diversity: The sociopolitical context of multicultural education* (4th ed.). Boston, MA: Pearson Allyn & Bacon.

Noble, J., Orton, M., Irlen, S., & Robinson, G. (2004). A controlled field study of the use of coloured overlays on reading achievement. *Australian Journal of Learning Disabilities, 9*(2), 14–22.

Novak, J.D., & Cañas, A.J. (2008). *The theory underlying concept maps and how to construct and use them (Technical Report IHMC CmapTools 2006-01 Rev 01-2008)*. Pensacola, FL: Florida Institute for Human Machine and Cognition. Retrieved from http://cmap.ihmc.us/Publications/ResearchPapers/TheoryUnderlyingConceptMaps.pdf

Ovando, C. & Collier, V. (1998). *Bilingual and ESL classrooms: Teaching in multicultural contexts* (2nd ed.). Boston, MA: The McGraw-Hill Companies, Inc.

Owen, O., & Sarles, P. (2012). Exit tickets: The reflective ticket to understanding. *Library Media Connection, 31*(3), 20–22.

Pajares, F. (1996). Self-efficacy beliefs in academic settings. *Review of Educational Research, 66*(4), 543–578.

Pajares, F., & Johnson, M. (1994). Confidence and competence in writing: The role of self-efficacy, outcome expectancy, and apprehension. *Research in the Teaching of English, 28*(3), 313–331.

Patrick, H., & Ryan, A.M. (2009). What do students think about when evaluating their classroom's master goal structure? An examination of young adolescents' explanations. *Journal of Experimental Education, 77,* 99–124. doi:10–3200/JEXE.77.2.99–124

Phelan, P., Davidson, A.L., & Cao, H.T. (1992). Speaking up: Students' perspectives on school. *Phi Delta Kappan, 73*(9), 695–704.

Pianta, P., Belsky, J., Vandergrift, N., Houts, R., & Morrison, F.J. (2008). Classroom affects on children's achievement trajectories in elementary school. *American Educational Research Journal, 45*(2), 365–397. doi:10.3102/0002831207308230

Pianta, R.C., & Stuhlman, M. (2004). Teacher–child relationships and children's success in the first years of school. *School Psychology Review, 33,* 444–458.

Putnam, J.W. (1998). *Cooperative learning and strategies for inclusion: Celebrating diversity in the classroom*. Baltimore, MD: Paul H. Brookes Publishing Co.

Ralabate, P. (2010). *Meeting the challenge: Special education tools that work for all kids*. Washington, DC: National Education Association.

Rappolt-Schlichtmann, G., Daley, S., Lim, S., Lapinski, S., Robinson, K.H., & Johnson, M. (2007). Universal design for learning and elementary school science: Exploring the efficacy use, and perceptions of a web-based science notebook. *The Journal of Educational Psychology.*

Rappolt-Schlichtmann, G., Daley, S., & Rose, L.T. (2012). Emotion and cognition are co-related: A conversation with Mary Helen Immordino-Yang. In G. Rappolt-Schlichtmann, S. Daley & L.T. Rose (Eds.), *A research reader in universal design for learning* (pp. 57–61). Cambridge, MA: Harvard Education Press.

Remillard, J.T. (2005). Examining key concepts in research on teachers' use of mathematics curricula. *Review of Educational Research, 75*(2), 211–246.

Rice, M., Kang, D.H., Weaver, M., & Howell, C.C. (2008). Relationship of anger, stress, and coping with school connectedness in fourth-grade students. *Journal of School Health, 78*(3), 149–156.

Robinson, G.L., & Conway, R.N.F. (2000). Irlen lenses and adults: A small scale study of reading speed, accuracy, comprehension and self-image. *Australian Journal of Learning Disabilities, 5*(1), 4–13.

Rose, D.H., & Meyer, A. (2002). *Teaching every student in the digital age*. Alexandra, VA: Association for Supervision and Curriculum Development.

Ruffin, T.M. (2012). Assistive technologies for reading. *Reading Matrix: An International Online Journal, 12*(1), 1533242X. Retrieved from http://www.readingmatrix.com/articles/april_2012/ruffin.pdf

Ryan, R.M., & Deci, E.L. (2000). Self-determination theory and the facilitation of intrinsic motivation, social development, and well-being. *American Psychologist, 55,* 68–78.

Sander, J.B., Sharkey, J.D., Olivarri, R., Tanigawa, D.A., & Mauseth, T. (2010). A qualitative study of juvenile offenders, student engagement, and interpersonal relationships: Implications for research directions and preventionist approaches. *Journal of Educational and Psychological Consultation, 20,* 288–315.

Santangelo, T., & Tomlinson, C.A., (2009). The application of differentiated instruction in postsecondary environments: Benefits, challenges, and future directions. *International Journal of Learning and Teaching in Higher Education, 2*(3), 307–323.

Scieszka, J. (1996). *The true story of the three little pigs.* New York, NY: Puffin Books.

Schmoker, M. (2004*).* Tipping point: From feckless reform to substantive instructional improvement. *Phi Delta Kappan, 85*(6), 424–438.

Scholes, R. (1989). *Protocols of reading.* New Haven, CT: Yale University Press.

Schwartz, B. (1990). The creation and destruction of value. *American Psychologist, 45*(1), 7–15.

Schwartz, D. (1999). The productive agency that drives collaborative learning. In P. Dillenbourg (Ed.), *Collaborative learning: Cognitive and computational approaches* (pp. 197–218). New York, NY: Pergamon Press.

Solan, H.A., Ficarra, A., Brannan, J.R., & Rucker, F. (1998). Eye movement efficiency in normal and reading disabled elementary school children: Effects of varying luminance and wavelength. *Journal of the American Optometric Association, 69*(7), 455–464.

Spooner, F., Baker, J.N., Harris, A.A., Ahlgrim-Delzell, L., & Browder, D.M. (2007). Effects of training in universal design for learning on lesson plan development. *Remedial and Special Education, 28*(2), 108–116.

Stiggins, R.J. (2008). *An introduction to student involved assessment for learning.* Upper Saddle River, NJ: Pearson/Merrill Prentice Hall.

Strickland, D.S., Ganske, K., & Monroe, J.K. (2002). *Supporting struggling readers and writers: Strategies for classroom intervention 3–6.* Portland, ME: Stenhouse.

Strobel, J., & van Barneveld, A. (2009). When is PBL more effective? A metasynthesis of meta-analysis comparing PBL to conventional classrooms. *The Interdisciplinary Journal of Problem-Based Learning, 3*(1), 44–58.

Storbeck, J., & Clore, G.L. (2012) On the interdependence of cognition and emotion. In Rappolt-Schlichtmann, G., Daley, S.G. & Rose, L.T. (Eds.), *A research reader in universal design for learning* (pp. 62–89). Cambridge, MA: Harvard Education Press.

Streeval, A., & Armstrong, H.A. (2009). *Industrial revolution project guide: Grade 9.* Retrieved from https://pantherfile.uwm.edu/edyburn/www/tic-tac-toe-ColumbusEastIN.pdf

Sunal, C.S., McCormick, T., Sunal, D.W., & Shwery, C. (2005). Elementary teachers candidates' construction of criteria for selecting social studies lesson plans for electronic portfolios. *Journal of Social Studies Research, 29*(1), 7–17.

Thomas, J.W. (2000). *A review of research on project-based learning.* Retrieved from The Autodesk Foundation web site: http://www.bie.org/images/uploads/general/9d06758fd346969cb63653d00dca55c0.pdf

Thomas, S.P., & Smith, H. (2004). School connectedness, anger behaviors, and relationships of violent and nonviolent American youth. *Perspectives on Psychiatric Care, 40*(4), 135–148.

Tovani, C. (2012). Feedback is a two-way street. *Educational Leadership, 70*(1), 48–51.

Tse, L. (2001). *"Why don't they learn English?" Separating fact from fallacy in the U.S. language debate.* New York, NY: Teachers.

Usher, E.L., & Pajares, F. (2006). Inviting confidence in school: Invitations as a critical source of the academic self-efficacy beliefs of entering middle school students. *Journal of Invitational Theory and Practice, 12,* 7–16.

Valkanova, Y. (2004). Enhancing self-reflection in children: The use of digital video in the primary science classroom. *Journal of eLiteracy, 1,* 42–55.

Vega, V. (2012). *Project-based learning research review.* Retrieved from the Edutopia web site: http://www.edutopia.org/pbl-research-learning-outcomes

Whitted, K.S. (2011). Understanding how social and emotional skill deficits contribute to school failure. *Preventing School Failure, 55*(1), 10–16.

Wiggins, G. (1990). *The case for authentic assessment.* Retrieved from ERIC database. (ED328611)

Williams, J. D. (2006). Why kids need to be bored: A case study of self-reflection and academic performance. *Research in the Middle Education Level Online, 29*(5), 1-17.

Williams, J., Evans, C., & King, L. (2012). The impact of universal design for learning on lesson planning. *The International Journal of Learning, 18*(4), 213–222.

Yussen, S. (Ed.). (1985). *The growth of reflection in children.* Orlando, FL: Academic Press.

Zelazo, P. (2000). Self-reflection and the development of consciously controlled processing. In P. Mitchell & K. Riggs (Eds.), *Children's reasoning and the mind* (pp. 169–189). London, England: Psychology Press.

Zimmerman, B.J., & Bandura, A. (1994). Impact of self-regulatory influences on writing course attainment. *American Educational Research Journal, 31*(4), 845-862.

Zimmerman, B.J., Bonner, S., & Kovach, R. (1996). *Developing self-regulated learners.* Washington, DC: American Psychological Association.

INDEX

References to tables and figures are indicated with *t* and *f*, respectively.